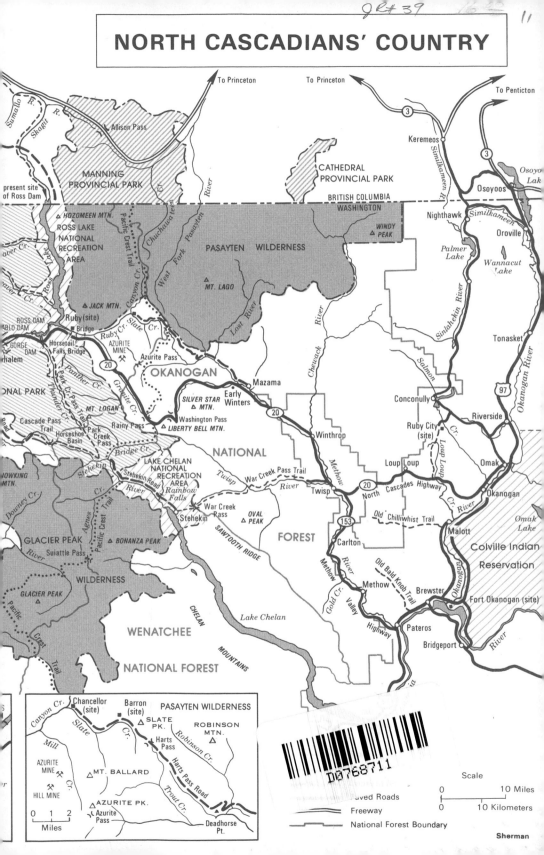

NORTH CASCADIANS' COUNTRY

To Princeton

To Princeton

To Penticton

3

Keremeos

Sumallo R.

Skagit R.

Allison Pass

Osoyoos Lake

MANNING PROVINCIAL PARK

present site of Ross Dam

CATHEDRAL PROVINCIAL PARK

BRITISH COLUMBIA
WASHINGTON

3

Osoyoos

HOZOMEEN MTN.

ROSS LAKE NATIONAL RECREATION AREA

Chuchuwanteen Cr.

West Fork Pasayten River

PASAYTEN WILDERNESS

WINDY PEAK

Nighthawk

Similkameen

Similkameen R.

Oroville

Palmer Lake

Wannacut Lake

er Cr.

ver Cr.

Ross Cr.

Ross Lake

MT. LAGO

Pacific Crest Trail

Lost River

Tonasket

Sinlahekin River

JACK MTN.

Ruby (site)

Canyon Cr.

Slate Cr.

Ruby Cr.

Bridge

ROSS DAM
ABLO DAM

Chewack River

Chewack River

Salmon Cr.

97

HORSETAIL Falls Bridge

GORGE DAM
halem

Azurite Pass

AZURITE MINE

OKANOGAN

Mazama

Conconully

Riverside

Panther Cr.

Granite Cr.

20

Early Winters

SILVER STAR MTN.

Ruby City (site)

Loup Cr.

Omak

ONAL PARK

Thunder Cr.

Park Cr. Pass Trail

MT. LOGAN

Washington Pass

20

Winthrop

Methow

Loup Loup

Okanogan

Cascade Pass Trail

Rainy Pass

LIBERTY BELL MTN.

Okanogan River

Horseshoe Basin

Park Creek Pass

Bridge Cr.

NATIONAL

20

North Cascades Highway

Malott

Omak Lake

OWKING MTN.

Stehekin

LAKE CHELAN NATIONAL RECREATION AREA

Twisp

War Creek Pass Trail

River

Twisp

153

Old Chilliwhist Trail

Colville Indian Reservation

Downey Cr.

Agnes Cr.

Stehekin Road

Rainbow Falls

River

War Creek Pass

Stehekin

OVAL PEAK

FOREST

Carlton

GLACIER PEAK

Suiattle Pass

BONANZA PEAK

Pacific Crest Trail

SAWTOOTH RIDGE

Methow River

Old Bald Knob Trail

Methow

Brewster

Fort Okanogan (site)

WILDERNESS

GLACIER PEAK

Gold Cr.

Valley

Pateros

Pacific Crest Trail

CHELAN

Lake Chelan

Highway

Bridgeport

River

WENATCHEE

MOUNTAINS

NATIONAL FOREST

PASAYTEN WILDERNESS

Canyon Cr.

Chancellor (site)

Barron (site)

SLATE PK.

ROBINSON MTN.

Slate Cr.

Mill Cr.

Robinson Cr.

Harts Pass

AZURITE MINE

MT. BALLARD

Harts Pass Road

HILL MINE

AZURITE PK.

Trout Cr.

Azurite Pass

Deadhorse Pt.

0 1 2
Miles

Scale

0   10 Miles

0   10 Kilometers

▬▬▬ ved Roads

▬▬▬ Freeway

▬▬▬ National Forest Boundary

Sherman

The North Cascadians

The North Cascadians

JoAnn Roe

1980
Madrona Publishers
Seattle

Published by
Madrona Publishers, Inc.
2116 Western Avenue
Seattle, Washington 98121

Library of Congress Cataloging in Publication Data

Roe, JoAnn, 1926-
The North Cascadians.

Bibliography: p.
Includes index.
1.   Cascade Range — History.   2.   Frontier and pioneer life — Cascade Range.
3.   Mountain life — Cascade Range — History.   I.   Title.
F897.C3R63   979.7′7   80-21620
ISBN 0-914842-49-8

I dedicate this book to my beloved husband,
Ernie Burkhart,
who has enjoyed the research as much as I.

Acknowledgments

Margaret Ziegler and other reference librarians, Bellingham
     Public Library.
Every one of the Omak librarians.
Susan Barrow, Whatcom Museum of History & Art, for her
     consistent encouragement, as well as Pat Fleeson.
Ray Steiger of the U. S. Forest Service for making my research
     of ranger lore so pleasant.
All of the members of the North Cascades Highway Associa-
     tion, particularly Sig Hjaltalin.
Galen Biery, coauthor of books on Bellingham history with
     Dorothy Koert.
All of the members of the Okanogan Historical Society, who
     have painstakingly preserved pioneer records.

Contents

Illustrations   Follow page *86*

The North Cascadians

1

The North Cascadians' Country

On September 2, 1972, the North Cascades Highway was opened, joining for the first time the east and west portions of northwestern Washington. Man had begun to explore space by then, yet had not touched parts of the rugged North Cascade Mountains, which stretch unbridged from the Hope-Princeton Highway, thirty miles north of the Canadian border, to Stevens Pass, sixty miles south of the international line. Not that he hadn't tried.

Since the time of Alexander Ross, a white man who crossed the mountains in 1814, North Cascadians had probed the mountains to determine what mineral riches or verdant valleys might be hidden in them. Some found gold but were frustrated by realizing no profit, partly because there was no practical transportation to smelters. Isolated homesteaders fought for ways of moving livestock and dairy products to distant consumers, so they might continue to live in the fertile valleys that thrust deep into, but never through, the North Cascades. Seeking electrical power for the industries developing along Puget Sound, the dam builders sought to control the Skagit River. But before raising dams, they were forced to build railroads for access to construction sites. Born of the United States government's desire to control and preserve large tracts of forest lands for posterity, a new agency, the Forest Service, sent rangers into the North Cascades with little more than axes and shovels to protect the forests, even as lumbermen strove to harvest the giant trees, building short roads and railroads to get them to market.

They were sturdy and violent men and women, these North Cascadians. If the mountains wouldn't surrender trails, they clawed their way into the canyons by hanging onto the sides of cliffs and crawling over rocks. When snows came to bury the high passes and valleys, pioneers supplied their mines by dog sled or by backpackers on snowshoes. Because mountainsides were too steep to permit horses and wagons to gather and transport felled logs, resourceful men conceived and manufactured new devices to meet their peculiar needs.

The North Cascades are not the highest mountains in the United States but are possibly the most vertical, gaining them the nickname of the American Alps. Rising abruptly from steep-sided valleys to 8,000 to 10,000 feet, the peaks are often capped by glaciers, which spawn brawling streams that tumble down both sides of the range, feeding a rich river system for all of Washington State — the Skagit, Nooksack, Methow, Okanogan, Suiattle, and the mighty Columbia.

There are no rigid boundaries for the North Cascades. Rather, the term refers to the northernmost part of the Cascade Range that extends north and south through the states of Oregon and Washington. Covering at least three and one-half million acres, the North Cascades stretch from north of the international border to an arbitrary point somewhere near Lake Chelan. The foothills spill westward to Bellingham, ninety miles north of Seattle on Puget Sound, and eastward toward the broad mesas beyond the Columbia River.

The range has two faces. Drenched by heavy rains from clouds that frequently move eastward from the Pacific Ocean, the western slopes are clothed with dense thickets of berry bushes and underbrush beneath towering trees — especially Douglas fir, which thrives in the damp river valleys. Influenced by winds coming from coastal waters fed by the warm Japanese Current, the western foothills and valleys enjoy a mild climate with little winter snow at sea level, but with heavy and wet snows in the higher mountains. Having spent their moisture upon the western slopes, clouds move benignly above the eastern slopes of the North Cascades, leaving them fairly dry — indeed, almost desertlike at lower elevations. Pungent forests of Ponderosa pine grow wherever roots can cling to the rocky soil of rugged hillsides or high plateaus. Unaffected by the moderating coastal winds, the eastern slopes suffer sharp seasonal variations of heat and cold.

Because man has left so little imprint upon the mountains, animals and birds live unafraid and mostly unhunted. There are cougars, mountain goats, deer, elk, an occasional moose, black bears, and, on rare occasions, grizzlies, which wander down from Canada. Bald and golden eagles nest in the snags and branches of the soaring conifer forests.

Today most of the high North Cascades country has been set aside for the public to enjoy as a national park, recreational area, wilderness, and land managed for multiple use by the Forest Service. The debris of man's mining efforts, largely fruitless, is being carted away. After a century and a half of exploration, the North Cascadians have succeeded permanently only in building the highway and the dams and living in scattered groups in the foothill valleys. The saga of these pioneers was a part of the westward movement of Americans, an exciting segment of the history of settlement in the Pacific Northwest.

Having resisted most of man's efforts at exploiting their resources, the North Cascades are returning to the pristine state that existed before the arrival of white men (Indians seldom ventured into the awesome high country).

Because of the sharp, uneroded appearance of their peaks, the North Cascades once were thought to be new mountains. Actually, nature has been at work sculpturing and rearranging the mountain range from the Cambrian Era (a period 500 million years ago, when all of North America was low-lying and the oceans spread across the land three different times) to the present day, when glacial activity and volcanic eruptions still continue. The range began as a trench filled with eroded materials, which were squeezed upward and downward by the pressure of land moving on either side of them. During successive eras, submarine volcanoes boiled through fissures in the sea floor, bringing molten rock to the surface and depositing it on top of older rocks in the continuing creation of a mountain range. During the final major upheaval that marked the formation of North America, between thirty and eighty million years ago, a time when warm-blooded animals began to appear, there was a violent explosion within the North Cascades that disgorged the very footings of the range lying close to the earth's core. Literally blown through space, the ancient materials were deposited high on Church and Larrabee mountains, near Mount Baker, on top of newer rock. Fifty miles away, a different type of molten material was deposited on Liberty Bell Mountain, Golden Horn Peak, Mount Silverstar, and others — golden-orange rocks that, solidifying in jagged ridges, form a dramatic silhouette against the intensely blue sky above Washington Pass.

Since then, periodic slippages have occurred, tilting the mountain masses. At one time, a ripple of the earth's crust rolled through and gently folded the entire range, leaving formations of rock that appear like ribbon candy. Glaciers poured off the peaks into the valleys, reaming out canyons, crossing paths with the giant continental glacier that surged over the Methow Valley to scour out Lake Chelan, a lake fifty miles long that extends four hundred feet below sea level. When the Ice Age ended, melting ice flooded a series of lakes between the Cascades and the Olympic Mountains, sending the waters through the land mass to form the Strait of Juan de Fuca and admit the sea. The ancient Columbia, a super-river many miles wide, poured over a gigantic waterfall in eastern Washington, forcing its way through the mountain range past today's Portland.

Even in more recent centuries the mountains have not rested quietly. An old Indian legend relates the story of a battle between two mountains, thought to be Mount Baker and a volcano in Idaho, during which two gods threw rocks at each other. Mount Baker erupted in 1843, throwing ashes as far as the Skagit Valley. Its cone still steams, with significant bursts of activity recorded in 1854, 1858, 1870, and 1975. In 1900 an earthquake raised a portion of the south fork of the Nooksack River about seventy feet above its previous level, opening seams through which gravel was forced into ledges ten and twenty feet high, without disturbing adjacent land surfaces.

Such inexplicable happenings helped to foster the belief among some foothill Indians that the white peaks were the home of the gods. Other Indians, especially the Okanogans, believed that a race of wild men lived in the high country, ready to kidnap any trespassers. Indians of the upper Skagit believed that Sauk Mountain near Rockport, known to the Indians as Mount Penalomah, was the home of two opposing spirits — one the great parent of the Creator, whose purpose was to lead the Indians into righteousness, the other an envoy of the prince of darkness who tried to destroy them. Looking at the forbidding mountain, a dark-colored peak devoid of growth and shaped like a pyramid, it is easy to believe that contests between these two forces are responsible for the black clouds and gray fogs that hang over it. Flashes of forked lightning and claps of thunder roll around it during summer storms. When an important decision was pondered, the Indians looked at Penalomah. If an eagle circled the crag on poised wing, the answer was favorable; if it fluttered its wings, it was not. The mountain was not blamed for predictions that did not come true; instead, the observer was punished for inattention.

Because the Indians usually passed their history from generation to generation orally, and the facts tended to vary somewhat with the teller, it was from the diaries of two white men — Alexander Ross and Henry Custer — that the curtain raised slightly on the mysterious North Cascades.

Alexander Ross, a lifetime trapper, came to Fort Okanogan on August 31, 1811, as clerk for the Pacific Fur Company. He had only his dog for company. "Fort" was an imposing name for the shoddy sixteen-by-twenty-foot shack, but in the first year of Ross's employment he procured 1,550 beaver pelts worth £2,250 sterling. In 1814, after vying with the North West Company for three years, Pacific Fur encountered such difficulties with its supply lines that it partly sold to North West and partly defaulted on its holdings in the Okanogan country. Ross switched allegiance to become the factor for North West Company at Fort Okanogan, responsible not only for gathering furs, but also transporting them safely 300 miles to market at Astoria.

Since transportation by river was through rapids and along lands occupied by sometimes hostile Indians, Ross eyed the North Cascades to the west and wondered if there was a direct route across them to Puget Sound. Red Fox, chief of the Okanogans, said he and his braves had been to the Great Salt Lake, as he termed the Pacific Ocean, in fifteen days' travel time. With only the vaguest of directions from the old chief, Ross and three Indian guides set out in July, 1814, to find the trail. Their trip took them along the Okanogan and Columbia rivers to the mouth of the Methow, then up the Methow Valley and Twisp River. There were times that Ross severely doubted the accuracy of his instructions. There was no path to be seen, but the chief guide insisted that they were headed in the right direction.

The small group pushed through broken country south of Washington Pass, descended along Bridge Creek to the Stehekin River, then ascended to Cascade Pass, discovering a stream (the Cascade River) that flowed west instead of east. Weakened by fatigue and exposure in the chilly heights of the pass, the chief guide became so ill that Ross was forced to send him back toward the fort with a second Indian. Convinced that he could descend to the sea, Ross pressed on with the third, very reluctant guide, who was apprehensive about being in the high country, the dwelling place of the gods. Following the Cascade River toward the Skagit, the two men encountered a full-fledged hurricane. The southwestern sky grew black, and there was a terrifying, mysterious noise like, according to Ross's diary, "a heavy body falling from a great height." As the noise came closer, big cedar trees bent down like saplings. The storm swept before them, mowing down everything "like grass before the scythe." The violence of the storm only strengthened the Indian's conviction that he was trespassing. While Ross slept that night, he slipped away to work his way back to Okanogan. As Ross dared not proceed alone, he also turned back and caught up with the three Indians, returning to Fort Okanogan, from which the four had set out thirty days before.

Over four decades passed before the mountains were penetrated again. Territorial Governor Isaac Stevens commissioned Captain George McClellan in 1853 to search for a wagon or rail route, but he only skirted the eastern edge. From 1857 to 1859 the United States Government sent a survey party to mark the international boundary on the forty-ninth parallel. Beginning in the summer of 1859, a member of this party, Henry Custer, made three sweeping explorations into the North Cascades near the Skagit River, recording his impressions in a forty-seven-page report to the Boundary Commission. Custer provided a glimpse into this unexplored land — an alpine wilderness of peak upon peak, extending eastward as far as he could see, broken only by precipitous, heavily-wooded river valleys.

Leaving his survey camp at Chilliwack Lake, a mile north of the border, Custer struggled through thick underbrush and towering fir and cedar trees to the top of Copper Mountain. From there he could see Mount Baker and Mount Shuksan to the south, perceiving the latter, ". . . not as an isolated peak, but as an immense perpendicular wall many thousands feet elevated above the massive piramidical base of the Mt." He complained about the difficulty of penetrating the thorny thickets of the western slopes:

. . . you have to work with hand & foot, to break, or hold away the very elastic twigs of the bush, which if not careful will give you such a lesson, you will not soon forget. Add to this a most disagreeable thorny plant with large leaves & red berries [devil's club] . . . and an intolerable swarm of mosquitoes.

But after treating his wounds and resting a few days, Custer set out a second time, retracing his earlier trail to Copper Mountain, then exploring eastward between Tapto Lakes and Whatcom Pass to the Skagit River. At the pass, Custer was awed by the magnificence of the Challenger Glacier in the Picket Range less than two miles south of him, writing in his diary:

Nothing ever seen before could compare. . . . All the glaciers . . . vanish before it into insignificance, in comparison with this closs [colossus] of glaciers. . . . Below it we see numerous cascades, hundreds of feet high, sending their dust like waters over the rocky pricipitous cliffs.

Custer's third and final trip was easier; on August 27, in an eight-man canoe paddled by Nooksack and Chilliwack Indians, he floated gently down the Skagit. As he approached Big Beaver and Ruby creeks, the current quickened and the Indians pulled into shore to avoid becoming caught in the rapids. Upon investigation Custer found that a fifteen-foot waterfall tumbled into a gorge a short distance ahead. Turning back, Custer and his men cached the boat while they explored the country east of the Skagit as far as "a river," probably the Pasayten, then retraced their route to the survey camp.

In his report given to the U.S. Boundary Commission much later, in May, 1866, Custer said he had explored more than 1,000 square miles which could now be mapped — no doubt an overoptimistic statement. Officials in Washington, D.C. read his report but shelved it. Significantly, both Ross and Custer had chosen pathways that were later followed by prospectors and road builders: Ross's trail became the Cascade Wagon Road, while part of Custer's route along the Skagit evolved into the Dewdney Trail from Fort Hope to the Skagit gold fields.

2

Gold, Coal, and Growing Pains

While the mountains remained largely unexplored, home-steaders began to nibble at the edges of Puget Sound, settling wherever it seemed possible to make a living. Twenty miles south of the Canadian border, along a swift-flowing creek terminating in falls that tumbled into Bellingham Bay, Captain Henry Roeder and Russell V. Peabody located a small mill in 1852 on lands given to them by the Lummi Indians. On nearby Sehome Hill in January, 1853, William R. Pattle and two associates filed donation claims for coal rights. Roeder, too, filed a claim on Sehome Hill in the fall of 1853, when two of his employees, Brown and Hewitt, discovered black "rock" beneath an uprooted tree.

Pattle's group sporadically mined coal by hand, abandoning its claim in 1859, but the enterprising Roeder mined sixty tons of coal in the winter of 1853–54 and transported it to San Francisco by ship, where it sold for sixteen dollars a ton. Seeking to sell the mine as well, Roeder sent Brown along with the coal; Brown readily found buyers, Fauntleroy, Calhoun, and Benham, who organized the Bellingham Bay Coal Company. For reasons never fully explained, Brown kept the $18,000 proceeds and headed for Denver, where he founded Brown's Palace Hotel, a famous and successful landmark.

On March 9, 1854, the handful of settlers living in the far northwest corner of the United States organized Whatcom County out of lands today designated as Skagit, San Juan, and Whatcom counties. Three years later, the county officials adopted a resolution for construction of a "Noot-sack* Road, not less than six feet wide," from Whatcom to a point on the Nooksack River near Everson — a decree which could be construed as the first effort to build a cross-Cascades road. Little did anyone know then what significance this trail would have.

Awakening one April day in 1858 to find a strange schooner anchored offshore in Bellingham Bay, Whatcom settlers watched as the ship disgorged its passengers. From the new arrivals, they learned for the first time that gold had been discovered in Canada. Prospectors working west along the Thompson River to the Fraser River had found gold south of the confluence of the two streams. Historian Hubert H. Bancroft estimated that, because the California mining boom was waning, 31,000 people left the San Francisco area between May and July for the Fraser. The author of *History of Washington*, Clinton Snowden, calculated that 75,000 to 100,000 gold-seekers came through the state in 1858. Pioneer Edward Eldridge remarked that at one time he counted seven ocean-going steamers and thirteen square-rigged sailing ships anchored in Bellingham Bay.

Maps showed Bellingham to be the closest point from which to go overland to the Fraser River, but such a trip was not easy. The sun's rays scarcely penetrated the virgin timber, much of it Douglas fir that stood as high as 150 feet. Men became lost, fell into marshes, and some drowned crossing the swift Nooksack River. Rushed into completion on May 18, 1858, by Whatcom County — with some volunteer help from miners — the little, rough Nooksack Trail was overused and soon became a bog. It clearly had to be improved and extended. A. M. Poe, first surveyor and engineer to locate in the Northwest, was hired to survey a route from Bellingham to the Fraser about twenty miles west of Fort Hope. Waiting miners, who were housed in tents along five miles of Bellingham Bay, from Chuckanut Bay to Squalicum Creek, pitched in to help build the new road.

Alarmed by the numbers of prospectors coming into the

*According to the Nooksack Indans, their name has been spelled many ways: *Nooksack, Noot-sack, Nut-sack*, etc.

Northwest via Whatcom County, Canadian authorities sought to divert the supply trade into their own ports by requiring men to obtain licenses in Victoria before searching for gold in Canada. From there the logical route to the gold fields would be to the mouth of the Fraser, probably past the Hudson's Bay Post. Unfortunately for the gold-seekers, the winter of 1858 was a killer, with unusual cold, snow, and ice. At Bellingham, the highest tides on record swept downed logs against the flimsy wharf. Miners drifting south from Canada painted gloomy pictures of scanty supplies and scantier gold, rugged country, grizzly bears, and shoulder-deep snow. The dearth of bonanza reports slowed the influx of prospectors, and the boomtown population along Bellingham Bay melted swiftly away.

Still, whenever men gathered at the saloons to swap stories, they wondered whether there was gold in the mountains above Bellingham. One tale persisted of gold on the Nooksack River. In midsummer, in 1858, prospector William Young flashed two gold nuggets he claimed came from a hole twelve miles north of the river near Sumas.

Intrigued by the stories, in August, 1860, five men, John Tennant, John Bennett, Frederick F. Lane, William Wood, and George Cagey, left to explore the Nooksack. They went almost due east from Bellingham, spending an agonizing five days of travel through heavy forest and over steep hills to the South Fork. Having found only slight traces of gold, they hired two Indians to transport them to the junction of the South and Middle forks — a dangerous trip through roaring rapids for seven men and a dog in an overloaded dugout. Exploration of the Middle Fork was also fruitless.

It would be twenty years before there was renewed interest in gold. In that time the settlements along Bellingham Bay — Whatcom, Fairhaven, New Whatcom, and Sehome, which later combined to become Bellingham — found it difficult to survive. Tall timber, which covered all of Whatcom County, made overland travel arduous and discouraged farming. The prospectors were gone. Because of the lessened activity, steamers called less frequently.

Only two industries kept the area alive. The Whatcom Milling Company sawmill, first established by Roeder, continued to operate but was crippled and closed by a major fire in 1873. Glow from the flames was visible for miles, attracting settlers to help with the firefighting, which consisted only of primitive bucket brigades. The mill was lost. On the docks 100,000 feet of finished lumber was saved by a valiant crew, most of them Lummi Indians, who stood waist-deep for hours in the chilly water passing the buckets along. The mill was reopened in the 1880s.

The area's other industry, the Bellingham·Bay Coal Company, after drifting along for six years, was reorganized in 1859 and capital raised for constructing proper mining facilities. Subsequently leased to William Moody and his partner Sinclair, experienced miners, the mine employed about one hundred men at the Sehome vein — half of them Chinese. An old story relates that most of the Chinese were drowned during a flooding of the shaft, but that seems unlikely, as they were usually employed outside on the coal dump. Mostly of English and Welsh ancestry, the miners lived dismally below ground. With a high sulphur content, the coal was subject to spontaneous combustion. Gases in the shaft were so heavy that it was impossible for workers to stay down for long. Nevertheless, Sinclair and Moody reportedly grossed $300,000 during their first year of operation — enough to warrant the purchase of three freighters for hauling coal to customers in San Francisco. Production continued satisfactorily until 1874, a year that seemed to be jinxed. In January, when the temperature sank to five below zero, workers refused to load or unload ships. Two months later, a huge pile driver — forty feet high with a hammer weighing two tons — was brought in to replace old pilings and build a second dock, but the hammer fell off the pile driver and buried itself deep into the mud. It was recovered only with much difficulty and loss of time. The bad luck continued. During the summer a workman was crushed when slate fell from the roof of the mine; in September, a spring burst within the mine, flooding part of it. Worst of all, the vein of coal pitched deeper and deeper into the earth, making the coal less accessible. Despite further fires and flooding, the company continued to take out coal until December, 1877, finally giving up and removing the machinery in 1878. The miners left, deepening the depressed economic conditions around Bellingham Bay.

Between 1864, when President Lincoln signed a bill providing for a railroad from Lake Superior to Puget Sound, and 1888, when the railroad reached Tacoma, pioneer Edward Eldridge tried to convince planners that Bellingham ought to be the Puget Sound terminus of the railway. At that time Bellingham residents could only speculate about the existence of a pass through the mountains. The North Cascades appeared to be a wall with no door. As a further obstacle to cross-mountain railroad construction, the Methow Valley and Okanogan country belonged to the Indians until 1886, part of the Chief Moses Reservation from Lake Chelan to the Canadian border.

There was sufficient turmoil among these foothill tribes that, in 1879, the Army built a temporary post near present-day Bridgeport on the Columbia River, later moving it to Fort Spokane. Wanting to know whether it was possible for the coastal Indians to join the inland Indians of the Columbia River area in some future conflict, the Army, on August 1, 1882, sent an expedition led by Lieutenant Henry Hubbard Pierce to explore the North Cascades for a route to Puget Sound.

Much of his path was the same as that of Alexander Ross, although from his diary Pierce did not seem to be familiar with Ross's trip. Instead of going up the Twisp River, Pierce traversed the mountain ridge between the Methow Valley and Lake Chelan, passing through War Creek Pass, from which he could see Lake Chelan "in color like an artificial lake of thick plate glass, while Pierce River [the Stehekin] brought its clay-tinted water with many a winding down the narrow canyon that opened up to the north." He descended to the Stehekin and followed it up toward Cascade Pass, noting Rainbow Falls as he went, "a magnificent cascades, with a sheer unbroken fall of 300 feet." Because a driving sleet storm at the pass made it too slippery to get the pack stock up the steep slope, Pierce sent most of his party back toward

Fort Colville. He and a few men continued on into the Skagit Valley as far as Sterling, a logging camp twelve miles above Mount Vernon.

Pierce returned to the fort in September to report that the government need not worry about the clashing or cooperation of Indians east of the mountains with Indians west of the mountains. The terrain was too forbidding for easy communication.

On both sides of the North Cascades sporadic mining exploration continued for gold, silver, and coal. Concurrently, increasing numbers of homesteaders cleared the forests to provide farmland, caring nothing for prospecting. Some of these pioneer North Cascadians did begin to realize the value of the vast stands of virgin timber, especially in Skagit County.

3

The Skagit Valley Comes Alive

Except for steamer traffic, Whatcom County was virtually cut off from adjacent counties by the semicircle of mountains surrounding it: the Canadian Coast Range to the north, the North Cascades to the east, and the Chuckanut Mountains, which extended from the North Cascades to Puget Sound. Prior to 1883, when Skagit County was formed from part of Whatcom County, the latter also included the broad Skagit River Delta just south of the Chuckanuts and the narrowing valley that thrust more than seventy miles east into the wall of the North Cascades.

The Skagit Valley was largely bypassed by the gold rush of 1858, partly because it was easier for miners to travel by water to Bellingham Bay. Also, unfriendly Swinomish Indians had frightened off the earliest travelers along Swinomish Slough. In 1855, Colonel Isaac Ebey tried to homestead some land near the mouth of the Skagit River but was so threatened by the warriors that he established his farm on Whidbey Island instead — only to be beheaded two years later by the northern Indians.

The first Skagit settlements occurred at the edges of Puget Sound on Guemes Island and Fidalgo Island, the present-day site of Anacortes. About a dozen families also lived near the trading post of Swinomish, now La Conner, first built in 1867 by Alonzo Low, renamed later for Louisa A. Conner by her husband John. According to estimates in the *History of Skagit County*, published in 1906, there were probably no

more than fifty or sixty people in the entire county in 1870 —
most of them living near the Sound. Homesteaders on the salt
marshes of the Samish Flats had found that with draining
and diking the land produced bumper crops of grain and
potatoes.

Unfortunately, the Skagit River and its tributaries flooded
the flat fields during heavy rains, chiefly because the flow of
the river was blocked by two huge log jams. The lower one, a
half-mile long, just below today's town of Mount Vernon, was
believed to be a century old. The upper jam, above Mount
Vernon, extended more than a mile and was increasing in
length by a quarter-mile every three years. Sediment had
accumulated on top of the jams so deeply in places that brush
and trees grew there.

In 1874, settlers living in the flatlands petitioned Congress
for $25,000 to remove the jams, but an investigator sent to
assess the situation estimated that the removal would cost
four times that much. Tiring of governmental delays, the
Skagit settlers decided to do the job themselves and by December of 1874, almost half of the lower jam had been removed. The Snohomish County newspaper, *Northern Star*,
reported that men cut through up to eight tiers of jammed
logs, some three feet in diameter. For the volunteers it was
dangerous work. The constricted river was turbulent beneath
the debris, and there were treacherous holes in the
haphazardly jammed logs. One man fell into such a hole,
disappearing beneath the jam. David E. Kimble, a fellow
worker, happened to see the victim's hand clutching the air
from a watery opening downstream and plucked out the
half-drowned man.

As work progressed, pressure from the swiftly flowing river
caused the jam to "work," dislodging in 1877 a section estimated at five acres. Later that year, workers were able to open
a channel 250 feet wide in the lower jam, but the water remained so turbulent that travelers usually portaged around. It
took two more years before a channel only 120 feet wide was
opened; even then, drifting logs sometimes closed the gap. It
was almost 1900 before the two jams totally dispersed.

When the lower log jam had been opened to river traffic,

Harrison Clothier and E. G. English opened a general store on the banks of the Skagit River between the two jams. Saloons, restaurants, and hotels soon followed to form the hamlet of Mount Vernon, named for George Washington's Potomac home. That same year of 1877, Hazard Stevens sold his landholdings around Ship Harbor on Fidalgo Island to Anna Curtis Bowman, the first white woman to settle there. Stevens originally purchased this land on speculation, when it was rumored that a rail line from eastern Washington might be built over Ward's Pass, terminating at Ship Harbor. The railroad never materialized and Mrs. Bowman established a wharf, store, and post office to form the nucleus of a town, named in 1879 — Anacortes, a slurring of her maiden name, Anna Curtis.

Before 1875, few people lived in the Skagit Valley above Hamilton — a small settlement where small amounts of coal were being mined by Amasa Everett and others. In October, 1875, Everett sold his coal claim to Skagit-Cumberland Coal Company and with John Rowley staked gold claims near the junction of the Skagit and Baker rivers. For two years the men prospected on the river, finding only small amounts of gold. To keep themselves in groceries, they raised potatoes and split cedar into doors and oars, selling them to the settlers of the lower valley. Everett remained on his claim, but in 1877 the more restless Rowley joined a prospecting party to probe the upper reaches of the Skagit River. In the group were Otto Klement, Charles von Pressentin, John Duncan, and Frank Scott.

They went by canoe as far as the mouth of the Skagit Gorge, where impassable rapids barred the way. There they built a cabin and some crude sluices and started to prospect. Gleaning only placer gold, the discouraged men packed their tools and supplies over Sourdough Mountain to the junction of Ruby Creek and the Skagit River. There pannings proved much better, but winter had set in with its vicious storms and heavy snowfalls, forcing the men to leave the mountains and return to Mount Vernon to wait for better weather. Elated with their gold findings, the men found it hard not to talk.

On February 1, 1878, still stormy in the Cascades, the party returned to Ruby Creek without von Pressentin but with two new members. They found just enough gold to hold their interest. Cold, lonely, and bone-weary, they worked through 1878, ever hoping that the next hole would be the big strike. Klement wearied of the struggle and returned to the valley in early summer, but the rest stayed until late in the year, when snows again drove them out. Surprisingly, no other prospectors appeared in 1878, but when the group returned in 1879, they found a group of men led by Albert Bacon working at Ruby Creek. By April, Bacon had taken out gold dust worth $1,500, and Rowley's party about $1,000 — which they cashed in on their return to Mount Vernon later that month. The secret was out then; the fat was in the fire. During the balance of 1879 and early in 1880, gold-seekers, estimated at 5,000, rushed to the upper Skagit to prospect.

After learning of the discovery, James A. Power, editor of the *Puget Sound Mail*, joined a party of prospectors to make the steamer *Josephine*'s initial run up the Skagit since the opening of the upper log jam. Guests also included representatives of the *Bellingham Bay Mail* and the *Seattle Intelligencer*. Editor Power returned to report that the mines were extremely inaccessible — 140 difficult miles from La Conner.

Because more money was made in outfitting the prospectors than in the discovery of gold dust, Skagit stores in the lower valley prospered. As word of new finds on Ruby, Canyon, and Slate creeks spread, Bellingham — with its fortunes at a low ebb — wanted to become a part of the supply market. P. B. Cornwall, financier and president of Bellingham Bay Coal Company, owned a store in Sehome that was operated by E. L. Steinweg. The two men discussed getting a trail through from Bellingham past Mount Baker, but were hesitant to spend the necessary time and money until it was proved that the mines were rich enough to warrant the investment. In December, 1879, a large group of businessmen and investors held a meeting at Squire's Opera House in Seattle, where they urged the construction of a trail, collecting $1,500 on the spot toward obtaining a builder. A contract was given to Day Brothers & Cockrane of Mount Vernon to construct a trail through the Skagit Gorge for $1,650, but they were later to back out.

Port Townsend, at the mouth of the Strait of Juan de Fuca, hoped it might also get some of the supply traffic, and Major Van Bokelan of that town offered money to Captain Henry Roeder of Bellingham for construction of a trail. Because the latter was one of the pioneers struggling to save Bellingham from collapse, he accepted the offer. Since it was possible to approach the Ruby mines by using the Fort Hope-Dewdney Trail, Roeder sent out a reconnaissance party in early February, 1880, to see if this route could be improved for a supply road. The men returned in March to report that they had to turn back twenty miles short of Ruby, where the snow was fifteen feet deep. Still, they believed the route was practical.

Miners who took part in the search for gold during the winter of 1879–80 said that the snow was twelve to thirty feet deep around Ruby and Canyon creeks; even at sea level it was over two feet. Although snow and rain swelled the river and avalanches and mud slides roared down the steep slopes, miners continued to arrive by canoe, rowboat, homemade dugouts, and on foot. One canoe with twelve men tried to go through the gorge but capsized; ironically, the six who could swim and tried to make it to shore were drowned, while the others who could not swim and hung onto the boat were saved.

John R. Ryan, a miner who went to the Skagit on the *Josephine*, denounced the hesitation of suppliers to invest in trail-building. In a long letter to the *Bellingham Bay Mail* he pointed out the difficulty of backpacking sufficient supplies to make prospecting worthwhile, when essential mining tools alone averaged forty pounds per man. He reported that, when a man did bring supplies in two canoes down the Skagit River to Ruby, almost all of the miners were waiting for him. They eagerly bought everything at good prices: flour at five dollars per sack; bacon, thirty cents a pound; gum boots, ten dollars per pair; and shoes, five dollars per pair. In an angry letter, Ryan condemned the faint-hearted merchants:

> In this age of progress and enterprise it is to be regretted that ,your lordly merchants below will not forward provisions to the Skagit gold mines or at least to the head of canoe navigation. When a commendable enterprise is on foot, it seems to me that all ought to take a hand and forward it to its completion. The

question arises, will the Skagit pioneers of my time ever develop
the mineral resources of these mountains or will the task belong
to the people of a generation yet to come, and of a more advanced
and enterprising age. Merchants, what say you to this? If you
wish to see the gold veins of the Skagit valley tapped and developed, forward the provisions and we will send you the shining
dust.

There were at least two responses. An imaginative group in
Seattle suggested using hot-air balloons to supply the mining
camps. A colorful Bellingham man, Dirty Dan Harris, made
an individual effort to supply the mines. Eccentric but likable
Dan was a booze-runner, packer, sailor, fighter, and homesteader in Fairhaven. He carried on his various enterprises
clad in a greasy coat, an unbuttoned red flannel undershirt
that showed off his massive chest, homespun trousers of in-
definite age, a Charlie Chaplin hat, and no shoes. Recognizing
the dearth of fresh meat at the mines, he drove three cows all
the way north to Fort Hope, then down the river to Ruby.
Imagine his chagrin when he arrived to find that the miners
had no gold and no money with which to buy the cattle.

Harris was so angry that he declared he would drive them
home again, "by gawd!" The half-starved miners licked their
lips hungrily; the beef was right there and they meant to have
it. Cries went up to take the cattle by force. In a spirit of
compromise and self-preservation, Dirty Dan slaughtered
one animal on the spot and gave it to the miners, accepting
vague promises of future payment, then hastily drove the
others back north. He arrived in Bellingham with two tired
and thinner cows and no money.

Although the gold rush did not result in any permanent
mines, the needs of prospectors who traveled up the Skagit
Valley caused the formation of the towns along the river.
Amasa Everett's place on the Baker River, and David Batey's
homestead and store near Sedro Woolley became way stations or supply points. Clothier and English established a
major store in 1880 at Goodell's Landing or Newhalem.

A member of the original gold-seekers, Otto Klement,
abandoned prospecting and opened a trading post in 1881 at
Lyman, nineteen miles above Mount Vernon. The post con-

sisted of a store, post office, hotel, and saloon, all under one crude roof. (Codiscoverer of gold Charles von Pressentin had homesteaded in 1877 a few miles away at Birdsview.) During the winters, Klement's hotel was filled to capacity by miners and adventurers. The winter of 1882 was particularly severe. The Skagit River froze over from the Sound to the Gorge so solid that teams of oxen could cross it — a situation not seen in modern times. Since heavy snows made hunting impossible, the Chinese cook at Klement's decided to slaughter a hog that he had been fattening in a pen. Bored with confinement at the small hotel, the guests sat around drinking most of that particular night, discussing how to dispatch the doomed hog. In the morning, John Bieble finally volunteered to do the job and end the discussion. With a poleaxe he took a mighty swing at the poor hog, but chopped down a portion of the roof instead, barely nicking the animal, which promptly ran off into the woods. The half-drunk hotel guests trudged after him and shot the beast, but now — how to get a 330-pound hog back to the scalding kettle? They attached ropes to his legs and started dragging him back over the snow but became lost in the foggy woods and found they had tugged the carcass several miles in the wrong direction. Patiently they pulled the deteriorating hog back to the hotel.

By the time the men reached Klement's place, most of the hide had been rubbed off the animal. Undisturbed, they dumped the pig into a barrel of scalding hot water without considering how they would pull him out before he cooked to pieces. By the time they had chopped the barrel apart, removed the remains of the hog, and hung them up on stakes to cool, they were thirsty again and retired to the saloon for more liquor. During the night a pack of dogs got into camp and ate the whole carcass, leaving the hotel still without meat.

It was, indeed, a crude life and it took hard men to bear the rigors. The foot trail to the Ruby mines led along the Skagit Gorge on a ledge that often had little more than a handhold to prevent the traveler from plummeting into the river. At the Devil's Corner, a large rock made travel impossible; so after first traversing a rickety suspension bridge along the riverbank, the intrepid North Cascadians clambered over the rocks on a system of ladders.

In 1884, an enterprising individual named Captain Randolph appeared in the Gorge. Why he came is unknown, but after looking at the Devil's Corner, he decided he could improve the trail. The high cliffs had some crevices; by digging into the cliff walls, he was able to widen the trail into a passable foot path. His reasons were not philanthropic, it developed; Randolph built a cabin squarely across the trail. During the summer of 1884, anyone wishing to use the improved footway had to pay him fifty cents to enter his cabin on one side and exit on the other. History does not reveal when or why Randolph's holdup scheme came to an end; maybe he wound up in the river along with his cabin, both victims of an irate non-toll payer.

Another mountain man was John McMillan, who arrived on the Skagit in 1884 to pack for the miners and grow hay for sale. On a trip to Fort Hope, McMillan picked up a starving Indian-Negro girl along the trail, taking her back to his home on Beaver Creek as a common-law bride. Several years later he went on a trip to Seattle, leaving supplies for his family. Tiring of the big city, he returned earlier than expected, only to find that his wife's relatives had moved in. In a rage he drove them all away, even his wife and children.

When the Forest Service was established in 1905, rangers found McMillan's knowledge of the North Cascades so valuable that they employed him as a Forest Guard in the Skagit District. McMillan later moved to Seattle but, when he became old and sick, he requested to be taken to Beaver Creek to spend his last days and die there.

Prospectors who had become disenchanted with the difficult life in the gold diggings often stayed to work at logging. The *History of Skagit County* states that seventeen log camps existed in 1888 between Lyman and Mount Vernon. In response to the demand for mills, Mortimer Cook built a shingle mill in 1886 at Sedro (a misspelling of the Spanish word for cedar — *cedro*), the first mill on Puget Sound to ship shingles to the East Coast. He also constructed a wharf on the Skagit River to handle visiting freighters. Actually, Cook named his original settlement Bug, because he wanted to give the town a name no one else would copy, but Mrs. Cook and her friends objected so strenuously that he changed it.

In 1889, a rival town and mill were started less than a mile away by Philip Woolley, who had learned where the crossing of the Great Northern Railroad and the Seattle & Northern was to be. For almost a decade the two towns vied with one another for the business created by the logging, railroad building, and the Cokedale coal mines six miles northeast of Woolley. The competition extended even to celebration of the Fourth of July when, in 1890, Woolley raised a flag from the top of a pole 104 feet high. Not to be outdone, Sedro ran up a magnificent 226-foot cedar pole with a flag forty by sixteen feet, made by the ladies of the community.

Both towns were weakened by the depression of 1893 and by fires that destroyed parts of both business areas. In 1898, they decided to join forces to eliminate the waste involved in having two town governments. Unable to agree on a neutral name, the citizens decided on the awkward composite of Sedro Woolley.

Almost every settlement along the Skagit River had a shingle mill by 1890. There were the Sauk Timber Company at Sauk, the Hawkeye Mill and Rockport Mill at Rockport, the Anna Shingle Company below Moss Hill, the Hightower Mill at Birdsview, four mills at Concrete, and others. One of the earliest loggers in the upper valley was Henry A. Martin, who came from Minnesota. At first pioneer lumbermen like Martin dropped whole trees directly into the river, rafting them downstream to mills at Everett or Anacortes. When the timber next to waterways became depleted, loggers cut trees into shingle bolts, tree trunks four feet four inches long, a size that two men could handle. These pieces were piled onto a log sled and pulled to the river by a team of oxen or horses along a skid road, a track of logs spaced six or eight feet apart. The logs were lubricated by a boy who preceded each team with a can of grease, smearing each log. (Washington State Senator Fred Martin, Henry's son, got his start as a grease boy.) When the team reached the river, it rammed the sled against a barrier tilted in such a way that the sled rolled over and dumped the bolts into the river. Then men in canoes with pike poles guided the bolts to the shingle mill downstream.

The numerous shingle mills worked together to enable a logger to send his bolts to the mill of his choice. Here is how it worked: When the Van Horn Mill, for instance, wanted to buy logs, a runner first went up the river to spread the word, so that all loggers wanting to sell to that mill could put their branded bolts into the river. Meanwhile, the mill stretched a gin boom across the river as a barrier to stop the bolts; a gin boom was a string of heavy logs long enough to reach across the river, held by a cable to prevent its being swept downstream. When not in use, it was swung back upstream and fastened against the shore.

Not everyone believed in an individualistic type of life like the logger and miner; around 1890, all over the nation, small clusters of people were trying to exist virtually without money. The Utopian Socialists established cooperative communities everywhere, but man's innate selfishness doomed most of these efforts. In the Northwest a few socialists split from the main national body, formed the Brotherhood of the Cooperative Commonwealth, and declared:

> Our purpose is to readjust measures and systems to the changed conditions of the social and industrial life . . . to give the people industrial as well as political freedom.

The effort was recognized by such well-known socialists as Eugene V. Debs and Henry Demarest Lloyd. The founders of the Brotherhood taxed themselves and also required a membership fee of $160 per family, soon raising $10,000 to buy 200 acres of land in 1897 near the town of Edison on the Skagit-Whatcom border. G. E. "Ed" Pelton, leader of the first group of Northwest socialists, named the colony Equality from the title of a book by Edward Bellamy. Extensive buildings were constructed by the enthusiastic colonists: two large apartments, a barn, storeroom, printing office, root house, bakery, sawmill, dining room and kitchen, cereal and coffee factory, copper shop, blacksmith shop, public school, milk-house, and even an apiary. Significantly, there was no jail, no saloon, no police force. Food raising was the main project, and the fertile Skagit delta was generous in its bounty. The colony acquired a fishing sloop and added seafood to its diet.

All went beautifully until after 1900. Members lived in large apartments, later in individual homes. Each person was allowed to choose his occupation but also had to agree to work at other assigned jobs if he had spare time. All policy was decided at the frequent town meetings, which everyone over eighteen was required to attend. Equality's political publication, *Industrial Freedom*, was circulated nationally.

Because the colonists behaved themselves, their neighbors liked them even if their way of life was different. Everything was, indeed, utopian for about four years; then, in succeeding years of the new century, matters worsened. Ideological disputes turned the town meetings into impossible wrangles. Professing socialist fervor, freeloaders joined the colony to tap the abundant food and supplies. In early 1906, a fire set by arsonists destroyed several buildings, including the barn and most of the cattle inside. Declaring that taxes were delinquent and a reign of terror existed in the colony, a group of colonists petitioned the court in Mount Vernon to place the Brotherhood under receivership. The land was then sold, the assets distributed, the colonists scattered, proving the previously declared tenets of the national socialists — that cooperative living simply did not work.

But it was a young, raw country where men had to search for ways to live together, as well as for riches. Although the North Cascadians of Skagit County had not become wealthy from gold strikes, by the early twentieth century they had explored the limits of their valleys and ventured into the unknown mountain country to the east. As they struggled into maturity, realizing that their riches lay in the black delta soil and the dense timber, they would look eastward for a road to new markets in and beyond the Okanogan country.

4

Settlers and Gold in the Methow Valley

North central Washington remained the domain of Indians until, in 1886, the Methow Valley, formerly part of the Chief Moses Reservation, was opened to settlers. The miners came, too, because strikes of gold and silver were reported almost as soon as white men entered the valley; in fact, homesteaders found Chinese miners working the lower Methow River and the Columbia near Pateros when they came. The Chinese sometimes brought wives and families with them and built crude, comfortable homes in dugouts along the hillsides. The Chinese life-style was very different from that of the whites; the men went on binges of opium smoking about every two weeks, often joined by their women, who left the children unsupervised without apparent harm. After sleeping off the effects of the spree, the Chinese went diligently back to work. The Indians were suspicious of the Chinese; it was said that they did not like the half-Oriental children that resulted from occasional romances with Indian women. For whatever reason, around 1890 the Indians attacked the Chinese miners, killed several, and frightened the rest away.

Credit for discovery of gold in the mountains south of the Methow River is credited to a Methow Indian named Captain Joe, a scout for a government exploration party. In 1886, while searching for horses, Joe broke off a piece of odd-looking rock and later showed it to his superior officer, Colonel F. S.

28

Sherwood. When the explorers returned to Portland, Sherwood showed the rock to friends who verified his suspicion that it was gold-bearing ore, and the news touched off an exodus of prospectors to the Methow Valley.

Only small claims were filed most of the time. In 1887, J. M. Byrnes made the first strike within the valley on Polepick Mountain, a hill near today's Twisp, and called it the Red Shirt Mine. In 1890, a Mrs. M. Leiser made a strike nearby and sold it to J. S. Crockett, who opened up a ledge of quartz and crystallized limestone that held profitable amounts of gold and silver. A small settlement gathered around the mines, calling itself Silver.

The pioneer homesteaders ignored the gold and made their claims for farmlands. In the spring of 1886 Mason Thurlow came into the valley over the old Chilliwhist trail, gaining immortality as the first permanent settler in the Methow. Before 1888 settlers had to cross the Columbia River on rafts, usually provided by friendly Indians, or else take apart covered wagons and float across on the wheelless beds. To serve the newcomers, in 1888 Thomas L. Nixon started a steamboat line from the Rock Island Rapids to the mouth of the Okanogan River, with a boat called the *City of Ellensburg*. Once on shore, Methow-bound travelers went over the Chilliwhist or Bald Knob trails — both bad. A young woman who came to the valley over Bald Knob in 1891 wrote to Eastern friends describing her trip:

> The road was rough and at some points we had to get out of the wagon and walk over the steep, sliding grades. To keep the back end of the wagon from sliding off, a rope was tied to the rear, then held by Sel Medaris, who also was walking. . . . After climbing seven miles uphill from Ives Landing through Watson Draw and down Arkansas Hill before starting the long, steep pull up over Bald Knob Mountain, we stayed the night at the old Chevall place located at the base of the mountain between upper and lower French creek. During the following day we arrived in the valley near the old Metcalf place on the Methow River just below the town of Silver. Going up the valley we crossed the Methow . . . the crossing was made in a canoe which was attached to a cable stretched across the river.

Despite the difficulties, they came — hundreds of miners

and homesteaders. They lived in log cabins chinked with earth and found them more snug than the later frame homes. They survived the unforeseen cold of the winter of 1889–90 that killed most of their stock, and the terrible winter of 1892–93 when the snow was four feet deep on the flat. This was the year that Ulrich Fries, a pioneer who told of his experiences in a book, *From Copenhagen to Okanogan*, carried the mail from Brewster to Winthrop for six dollars and sixty cents per round trip — a three-day venture and a round trip of almost 150 miles. As winter wore on, conditions got so bad that Fries sometimes took a whole week to deliver his mail route, thus was on the trail constantly.

The mining claims that extended up the Twisp River seemed to be quite rich, but were not worked extensively because transportation to smelters was too costly. The discovery of gold on the Twisp River was made in 1884 by E. W. Lockwood, Ed Shackleford, and H. M. Cooper and called the Washington Mine. Other claims were the Oregonian group and the Consolidated Twisp Mining & Milling Company claims. Some of the more promising mines along the Methow River included the Highland Light, with the deepest shaft of all, 140 feet; the Paymaster, Spokane, St. Patrick, Chicago, and the Friday claims. The claims extended over the hills into Horseshoe Basin, a high valley below Sahale Glacier and Boston Peak, and along Doubtful Lake in Cascade Pass. The plat of claims between the Twisp River and Cascade Pass grew together so that they resembled a modern subdivision's lots.

With so much activity above Stehekin, the tiny settlement on Lake Chelan became an important supply port, and by 1889 a dozen families lived there. The long trail from Stehekin up to the Horseshoe-Cascade diggings was fairly gradual, but at 5,000 feet miners were able to work only a few months of the year because of the heavy snow. Switzerland-like Stehekin was also discovered by the tourists, as it was accessible by boat. Captained by Charles Trow, the *Belle of Chelan* steamed into use in 1889, followed by the *Omaha* in 1890, and in 1893, the *Stehekin* was commissioned; over one hundred feet long with a sixteen-foot beam, the *Stehekin* clearly was designed with passengers in mind. It sailed Lake Chelan for about ten years, carrying tourists, miners, freight, and mail. The *Chelan Leader* said that the ship boasted a commodious ladies' cabin, a gentlemen's smoking room, and two galleys with first-class equipment to serve meals to the passengers. The ladies' cabin was furnished with a grand piano, sofa, and easy chairs.

The tourists were bound for M. E. Field's hotel, originally built in 1892 and called the Argonault, renamed the Field Hotel. It was an inn of astonishing elegance for its remote location, three stories high, surrounded by a broad porch, and furnished tastefully to cater to a rich clientele. Field launched a widespread advertising campaign to lure vacationers to the North Cascades. In one of his ads, he said:

> One of the loveliest spots on Lake Chelan. Superb trout fishing. At the head of navigation. Surrounded by Alpine scenery. Only three miles from the famed Rainbow Falls, 300 feet high. The health and pleasure seekers' Mecca. Every attention shown to guests and rates reasonable.

The contrast of luxury hotel and miners' lives was stark. Only a short way from the hotel, life and death were seldom far apart. In 1895 a man named Hughey McKerver left Stehekin to prospect and did not return in September, a month later, as scheduled. Field organized a search party but snows closed in and the search was abandoned. A year later another prospector discovered Hughey's body, upon which a bear had been feeding. In reconstructing his grisly death, it appeared that the man had fallen or been caught in a fight with a bear. His leg was broken but he had put snowshoes on his hands and tried vainly to get out of the mountains.

In the Methow Valley just over the mountain, life was earthy. News of a dance or social event brought in lonesome men from incredible distances for one night of companionship. The *Big Bend Empire*, published at Waterville in the 1890s, describes a gala opening of a hotel in the town of Methow. Not only is it a picturesque glimpse of frontier life, but of the journalistic style of the time:

> Mr. and Mrs. Hawthorne opened hotel in Methow by extending a cordial invitation to all to attend the 1st dance on Squaw

Creek. There were a dozen or more ladies as fine looking and nicely dressed as you would meet in a New England city waiting for the word 'Honor Your partner,' which they did to the queen's taste, and the gentlemen looked wise and all slicked up with their six-bit overalls and hob-nail boots, they would remind you of a lot of Mormon Elders after prayer meeting. The music was furnished by Iceberg Bill from Manitoba, who played the harmonica with his mouth, the violin with his right and the bow with his left hand and came down on the new board floor with his two left feet in accordance with the music. Gilmour's famous band of New York would not be in it. They whirled until midnight when refreshments were served, and the way the corn-fed prospectors hid their ears in homemade pie would strike terror to the heart of a Mississippi native in watermelon season.

Sourdough Tom led the grand march with his military aspect and prepossessing appearance, spieling the good old-fashioned air "Jerry, go oil the cat." It would remind you of a horse coming home after being beaten. Look-out Jack was master of ceremonies, and conducted himself manfully. Senator Washburn favored the audience with a recitation entitled: "The Ups and Downs of Life in Grub Stake Canyon," which was the wind-up.

The Methow Valley frontiersmen were pranksters. Children always went along to dances, and younger ones slept happily on a cloakroom table among coats and bundles, while the dance went on. One night a couple of well-known characters, Dick McLean and Peter Bryan, crept into the cloakroom and changed around all the children's outer clothes; some parents got all the way home before discovering that they had picked up the wrong child.

The remote country had its share of characters. There was the Jumping Frenchman, a twitchy man who hired out with a team of horses to help covered wagons through the worst parts of the trails. He got his name because he moved so fast to do anyone's bidding. There was a hermit, Bill ("Dirty Bill") Waters, who never cut his hair or bathed. He was supposed to be a Princeton or Harvard graduate who spurned civilized life after an unhappy love affair. The only thing he liked was horses; he could walk up to the wildest ones and rub their necks. He was so lazy that he put his bed close to the stove so that he could replenish the fire without getting up. When any of the wild horses that hung around his cabin died, he just left them where they dropped.

At tiny Winthrop, Guy Waring and an associate, Milton Storey, recognized the inevitability of a saloon in town and opened their own, one that they could control and keep respectable. It was like no other in the West. Called the Duck Brand Saloon after Waring's cattle brand, it had such strict rules that one wonders how it attracted any customers. There were no chairs or tables, no gambling or "treating" of anyone, the bartender was allowed to talk only about the orders, and the bar closed every night at ten. Only the best liquors and fine imported tobaccos were sold, so maybe this made the restrictions bearable.

Guy Waring was one of Okanogan County's most colorful citizens, coming to Winthrop in 1891 to form the Methow Trading Company, with stores eventually at Twisp and Pateros. During the severe winter of 1892–93 his combination store and cabin burned and he and his family had to spend the winter in his brother's sixteen-by-twenty-foot cabin. Because the snow was too deep to paw aside, his horses were so starved they ate each other's manes and tails and chewed off all the pine branches within reach. Waring's post office had burned along with the cabin, and for a time it operated from the root cellar. When spring came, Waring rebuilt. Because he was the chief permanent resident of the area, he was called upon to serve as amateur doctor, among other things. One day a miner named Langer, cook at the Slate Creek Mine, accidentally shot himself in the leg. His fellow miners brought him to Winthrop, strapped to a board, over the Hart's Pass Trail. The nearest doctor lived sixty-seven miles away at Chelan and Waring sent a horseman to fetch him. The messenger found the doctor dead drunk and had to sober him up before he could ride. The bleary medic finally arrived at Winthrop, took one look at the miner's leg, and declared it had to come off. Langer begged Waring not to permit it, that without a leg he could never return to work. When the doctor would not consent to any other approach and left in a huff, Waring took a sharp knife and picked out all the loose pieces of bone and bandaged Langer up. Miraculously, the man's leg did not become infected and healed with only a slight limp. On another occasion Waring sewed together a man's finger that had been ripped off in a log-rolling accident — a type of operation that made headlines in the 1960s.

Winthrop today has a prominent sign on its main street that indicates Owen Wister, author of *The Virginian*, spent time there. Wister did spend time with Waring in 1892 and again in 1898 for his honeymoon; and it is believed that he used his experiences in the Methow as background material.

Despite mixed results from mining, prospectors continued to work the mountain passes and valleys. Lawrence K. Hodges, author of an engineering treatise, *Mining in the Pacific Northwest*, said that the first wave of prospectors was too inexperienced, that the smelters were too far away from the gold strikes. A five-stamp mill with one concentrator was erected on Squaw Creek along with two arrastres (an arrastre is a type of ore crusher). When it was completed, twelve tons of Paymaster ore that was run through the mill barely paid expenses, and forty-five tons milled at Charles Austinburg's arrastre resulted in *tailings* (materials left after refining) that yielded forty-five dollars and *assays* (gold realized) that ranged from twenty-three dollars to sixty dollars — an altogether backward situation.

In 1892, Alex Barron located a really valuable strike in Hart's Pass. Like hundreds of other prospectors, Barron was panning the streams, working his way eastward from Ruby Creek. The alert miner noticed that, as he got farther upstream, some of the gold seemed different from placer gold, coarser and of a different color. He reasoned that it had come from higher up in the mountain and sank exploratory holes along a 500-yard stretch. His persistence paid off with a strike right near the surface. Smitten more with the thrill of discovery than with the day-to-day work of mining gold, Barron promptly sold his claim to Eureka Mining Company of Anacortes for a reported $50,000 to $80,000. The company eventually extracted more than $300,000 in gold from this one claim. Barron, a boomtown complete with saloons, stores and crude housing for 2,500 people, mushroomed out of the steep-walled valley. Old-timers say that Alex Barron spent his poke in riotous living within a short time, returned broke to the same area and soon located the Beck claim (three miles from the original), which netted him another $75,000 to $100,000. A curiosity at the World's Columbian Exposition in Chicago in 1893 was a 400-pound chunk of ore taken from the Barron mine, which was transported by canoe most of the way to the Skagit River.

An entrepreneur instead of a miner, Colonel Thomas Hart came to Hart's Pass at the request of Barron in the 1890s and decided that he would build a road (giving his name to the pass and trail). He hired Charles Ballard, later a key owner of the Azurite Mine, to lay out a trail from Robinson Creek to Slate Creek on the opposite side of the mountain. It was not a trail for the faint-hearted. In one place the road literally was hung on the side of a sheer cliff by iron pins fastened into the face of the rock for eighteen feet, with planks placed on the pins to form a roadway. To the canyon below there was a sheer drop of 1,000 feet. This hair-raising section became known as Deadhorse Point after a pack horse slipped on the plankway and tumbled over into the chasm, pulling an entire pack train with him.

The road never was wide enough for a standard, wide-gauge wagon until well into the twentieth century; it was a narrow-gauge road, meant for specially-built wagons pulled by horses linked in tandem. It took steady nerves on the part of both horses and handlers to traverse the incredibly steep road. In places the freighters hooked block and tackle to iron rings fastened to trees and winched their wagons upward. Newt Williams, a freighter during the Slate Creek mining boom, spent one whole summer winching a heavy piece of equipment over Hart's Pass.

5

Gold Bubbles in Conconully and Ruby

Concurrent with the gold strikes in the Methow Valley and Hart's Pass, there were finds all up and down the eastern edge of the North Cascades — at Conconully, Ruby City, Loomis, and Palmer Lake. Mines with colorful names were opened — the Last Chance, First Chance, King Solomon's Mines, Lady of the Lake, Wooloo Mooloo, War Eagle, Tough Nut, Johnny Boy. The original Ruby Mine discovered by John Clonan, Thomas Donan, William Milligan, and Thomas Fuller in 1886 was actually one of the lowest-grade mines. There was more quantity than quality to the mines, though with proper development and less expensive supplies, some might have paid off.

The chief mining areas at Ruby and Conconully were twenty to twenty-five miles from the Okanogan steamers, farther yet from the Columbia. Prior to 1893 one shipping company owned both the Columbia River steamboats and the ferries across the Columbia and Okanogan rivers. In order to collect tolls from both ferries and the steamer, the steamships landed on the south side of the Columbia at Port Columbia, and goods had to be reloaded onto one or both ferries. In 1893 the now defunct town of Virginia City was platted about one-half mile south of present-day Brewster, promoted by Virginia Bill Covington and Francis Green. At that time the steamship company gave up its legal larceny and moved its terminal across the river to Virginia City. In 1896 the line was sold and the new owners built a brand-new port at

Brewster (then called Ives Landing), and Virginia City merchants moved their stores to the new location, abandoning the old town. Brewster handled most of the freight for the upper Okanogan from that time on.

The trails to the mines were little more than a pair of wagon ruts leading over the river flats, over part of the Chilliwhist Trail, including Three Devils Ridge where freighters had to hook logs onto their wagons to slow the descent, and on to Ruby City and Conconully.

Jonathan Bourne, Jr., of Portland, Oregon, bought the original Ruby and First Thought mines near Loup Loup and in 1892 organized the Washington Reduction Company to work them, building a concentrator and supportive installation that cost about $70,000. He also built a mile-long cable bucket tramway to transport ore from the First Thought to the plant. After producing about $40,000 in concentrates, the operation was closed in 1893 when the price of silver fell below a profitable level. The syndicate that developed the Fourth of July Mine extracted about 200 tons of ore and processed most of it at the smelters at distant Everett and Tacoma. It, too, closed in 1893, along with most of the mines along the eastern slope of the Cascades.

While they lasted, Conconully and Ruby City were two of the liveliest towns in sparsely settled Okanogan County. A letter written by Mathias Garigen to his sister in the East on October 14, 1888, provides an amusing insight into the attitudes of the miners:

> This is a healthy country. There has not been a natural death here since I came, and that is about one year and ten months, although there have been quite a number of deaths by accidents and otherwise. I know all the parties, the first man was shot with his own gun, the second was shot by accident although the shot was meant for another man. I helped to arrest him and take him to jail in Colville, Stevens County. The next was from drinking too much whiskey; the next man was shot and killed instantly. The murderer got free although the mob came very near shooting him. The next man while under the influence of liquor fell into a fire and burnt himself so badly that he died after two weeks of suffering; the next one after a hard spree rode in the hot sun until he went crazy and went in the brush and died. The others were killed blasting in a mine. The last man was shot accidently [*sic*]

by his own gun — he was riding along when his rifle fell to the ground, the ball went through his thigh and he bled to death. There have been three or four men shot but got over it and some cut with knives. You may think that I am telling you a story but I can tell you all of these men's names and how everything happened; it is not like it is in the east when men get to quarreling they fight it with their hands; here they carry a six shooter or a knife and do not use their hands to settle a dispute. I like this country and the people, although. . . .

Patriotism ran high in the early days, and on the Fourth both Indians and whites came with their fastest horses to race through the streets in celebration. Among the outsiders during one celebration was an Indian named Pocomaikin, known to be a bad *hombre*, for there was a warrant out for his arrest on a charge of murder. Pocomaikin came into remote Ruby City, confident that no one would know him, but he couldn't stay out of trouble. On the day of the races he perversely galloped down the main street, hugging close to the side of his horse, shooting indiscriminately. With men already mounted on their fastest horses, it was easy to get together a posse; the Indian continued to gallop right out of town and outdistanced his pursuers. Later he was killed in an unrelated incident near Malott.

The races heated even the tempers of respectable citizens. On another Fourth of July celebration Okanogan pioneer L. C. Malott raced his flashy buckskin horse against Rawl Sibert's steed and won; in a quarrel that ensued the disgruntled loser drew a knife and stabbed Malott; fortunately the wound was superficial.

When Okanogan County was officially separated into an entity out of Stevens County, Conconully and Ruby City vied for the honor of being the first county seat. In early 1888 Ruby City won the temporary appointment but on November 6 the official election showed a vote in favor of Conconully. The formidable depression of 1893 closed most of Ruby City, and people moved away leaving dwellings and stores vacant. Then came the vandals, vultures pecking away at the useful flotsam of the town, carrying off parts of buildings and machinery. At the turn of the century a fire destroyed three-fourths of the remaining structures, and by 1903 the rest had fallen into ruins or been reclaimed by the forest.

Conconully fared a little better and has a couple hundred residents still. Its early days were tenuous; before it was thirteen years old, it had been ravaged by fire, flood, and storm in separate catastrophes. In 1892 a fire started in a business building and, fanned by a stiff wind, ate up two blocks of buildings before it was stopped. Shortly after, the depression caused many residents to leave town. Finally, in 1894 a merciless flood destroyed forty-two buildings. Conconully lay in a basin with the normally placid Salmon Creek winding through town; above and to the east was Conconully Lake. For weeks it had been dry and pleasant, but on May 26 a cloudburst pelted the mountains above the town. A combination of heavy rain and melting snow swelled Salmon Creek into a "gullywasher" by the following day. First to see the oncoming torrent was William Shufeldt who was sitting on his horse in front of the Hotel Elliott, when he looked up the mountainside to see a flood coming down the canyon. Bearing down swiftly, the torrent of water, trees, brush, and even rocks weighing hundreds of pounds converged on the town. It ripped out tall trees, sending them end over end in the rushing water, then the creek momentarily dammed itself up with the debris.

The town had a few moments of respite. Shufeldt spurred his horse and galloped up and down, yelling for everyone to get out. People had time only to run for the highest possible ground, and some never made it before the dammed-up creek burst loose again. When the flood reached the valley floor, it widened but still was twelve feet deep when it plowed into the town, knocking buildings off their foundations as if they were toys. The water ran completely underneath the Hotel Elliott, and logs and debris swirled as high as the second story; but the structure stood, twisted and damaged but intact. The store of Moore, Ish & Company was torn to pieces; even a stone cellar was carried away and a heavy iron safe washed off, never to be found again. Some houses were carried along by the flood and deposited unharmed farther downstream. When the dazed residents assessed the damage, property loss was estimated at close to $100,000 — a lot of money in 1894.

Because the town was a supply center for the rich Scotch Creek Valley ranches, as well as the remaining mines, its residents patiently rebuilt. But nature still was not through with Conconully. In August, 1901, a violent thunderstorm rolled over the mountains surrounding the town and burned most of the forests around it, coming right to the edge of the settlement, but it survived to remain a sleepy crossroads town.

6

Revival of Bellingham

Linked with the Okanogan and Methow country by the mutual interest in an east-west railroad, Bellingham's pioneers continued to struggle for the privilege of being a sea-rail terminus; Edward Eldridge promoted the idea for fifteen years to the Northern Pacific, only to lose to Tacoma. City father Henry Roeder noticed a brief item in a newspaper about a Kansas cooperative colony that was searching for a site on which to settle, and wrote to them about the advantages of Bellingham Bay. The leader of the Washington Colony (as it became known), General M. A. McPherson, came to Bellingham and met with Roeder, a Mr. Utter, and Eldridge and was favorably impressed. In return for the donations of a millsite and a half-interest in the town of Whatcom, McPherson promised to bring at least one hundred families, to construct a new mill, a wharf, and fifty homes. However, the townsite of Whatcom was a maze of tangled claims derived from the original joint ownership of much land by Roeder and Russell V. Peabody, and the subsequent death of the latter, which left a chaotic legal situation for his heirs. Because of the need to make a definite commitment to the Washington Colony, Roeder contacted the numerous heirs and gained a verbal agreement from most of them to go along with whatever Roeder thought best. Negotiations were consummated with the Colony; and within a few months settlers began to arrive — not the hundred families promised, only about twenty-five. The group was undercapitalized but industri-

41

ous, and swiftly went to work to fulfill their commitments to the Bellingham group.

No sooner was the die cast than the Peabody heirs refused to formalize their verbal agreements. Legal disputes and accusations ensued, complicated by the purchase of Colony stock by new investors like J. H. Stenger, who bought a majority of the outstanding stock and later became virtually the sole owner of the Colony interests. The dispute had not been without heated tempers. In 1885 Stenger's newly completed residence was blown up by two men who used a powder cartridge in a five-gallon oil can, ignited by a long fuse.

Despite the problems, the arrival of the Washington Colony was the impetus that saved the Bellingham Bay settlements and stimulated a new boom. Northwesterners began to comprehend the value of the forests surrounding them, and mills other than the Colony Mill were built, including the Knox & Musser Mill.

Bellingham's Fourth of July celebration in 1883 was a magnet that attracted 1500 people to applaud the upturn in fortunes. Choirs sang, orators orated, the New Westminster, B.C., band tooted, and a canoe race with twelve entries drew keen interest (forerunner of the Lummi Stomish races of today). British Columbia Indians won the race and were feted by the local Indians in an encampment of about 300 tents on the tidelands below the bluffs of Whatcom. A freak accident almost triggered a battle. On the bluff stood an old Farragut cannon, used infrequently to salute visiting dignitaries and to mark special holidays. To honor the Fourth, the cannon was fired and it exploded, sending pieces of metal hurtling onto the beach below. A big fragment plummeted through a tent, killing one Indian man and wounding another. Startled and indignant, some thought the whites had fired on them purposely and cried for retaliation. Conferring with the whites, Chief Henry Kwina learned the reason for the tragedy and quieted his angry tribesmen. Sobered by the tragic turn of events, the celebrants took up a collection to defray the funeral expenses of the dead man, and to cover medical help for the injured one (he died later). It was a gloomy end to a joyful celebration.

Between 1882 and 1892 the population of Whatcom County jumped to about 3,700; citizens could talk of little else but railroads. The companies were so numerous that one needed a program to keep track of the cast of characters. Land bought on speculation was sold within days at a profit.

Backed by P. B. Cornwall, the Bellingham Bay and British Columbia Railway was the first to make its debut in 1882, amid much fanfare. The new company negotiated with the Canadian Pacific Railway for a joining and terminus on Burrard Inlet near Vancouver, B. C. Although the latter did not commit itself, the B.B. & B.C. started surveying northward. Also, in 1882, a party of railroad men came to fish in Lake Whatcom — at least that was their publicly announced purpose — but the fishermen included the vice president and the assistant manager of Northern Pacific Railroad, probably there in response to an invitation from Edward Eldridge. Thomas Canfield came along in 1883 with his Bellingham Bay Railroad & Navigation Company, which was to go north from Fairhaven to the Canadian border through Everson and Sumas. Survey crews also worked south through the Samish Valley toward Mount Vernon.

There were other companies, some of them transitory. A company called Puget Sound & Idaho Railroad came on the scene in 1884; but I. S. Kalloch, its promoter and an ex-mayor of San Francisco, joined forces with B.B. & B.C. The Northern Pacific and the Puget Sound Shore Railway Company proposed to build rail and telegraph lines to Bellingham from Seattle, and Eldridge still was working on Northern Pacific to make Bellingham a main terminus. By 1885 there were no rails in sight, only paper plans.

New business firms opened to serve the increasing population — pioneer businesses that survive today like Morse & Caldwell, forerunner of Morse Hardware Company. The towns along Bellingham Bay began to mature, partly accelerated by the great leveler — fire. In midsummer of 1885, a giant forest fire started at Lake Whatcom and burned over the hills to Bellingham Bay, gobbling up timber as far as the center of Whatcom. Like an insatiable beast, it turned north and destroyed houses, farms, timber, and livestock all the

way to Canada, where it finally burned itself out. Stunned
county residents poked through the ruins of their homesteads, comforting themselves with the realization that the
fire at least had cleared big sections of land. That same summer a fire destroyed Steinweg's store, the Washington Hotel,
and other buildings. The towns took on a more permanent
appearance because the new construction was of brick and
stone, or properly finished lumber, instead of rough clap-
boards. Not that Bellingham had become too much of a me-
tropolis; in 1886 there were complaints by residents that
cows with bells on their necks, which roamed the streets at
night, disturbed their sleep.

No pass for a railroad had yet been found through the formidable North Cascades, nor for a wagon road to serve the
reviving mines of the upper Skagit. Therefore, between April
and June, 1886, Banning Austin, C. E. and E. P. Chace, H. C.
Wells, W. E. Garrett, and William Thompson explored the
mountains, searching for a way across. After many fruitless
forays toward the big peaks of Mount Baker and Shuksan, the
party camped in June in a meadow above timberline, divided
the last of their rations, and considered whether or not to
abandon the search. After a good night's sleep, the men decided to try once more to find a pass. Moving upward through
the meadow, they discovered a notch in the mountain range
and passed through it. At the summit they could see the
Skagit River at last. The elated men named the break Austin
Pass, descended to the Skagit, and followed the old Dewdney
Trail north to Fort Hope and back to Bellingham. Although
the explorers then agitated for a road, maybe a toll road which
would pay for itself, no action was taken by county officials —
probably because there were more urgent road problems.
Citizens pointed out that the county roads were more fit for
boats than for wagons, and that a large salmon had been seen
swimming across Guide Meridian Road.

Railroad plans had been in the doldrums during 1885, but
in the summer of 1886 Canfield's line, the B.B.R. & N., received a charter from Congress that gave it the exclusive right
to build railroad bridges across all rivers north of Seattle to
the Canadian border. While the rail line hastened to comply,

the Seattle & West Coast Railway Company started laying rails from Seattle through Snohomish northward. It then merged with the Seattle, Lakeshore & Eastern Railway, which completed the railroad to Sumas near the Canadian border by 1891, when it was purchased by the Northern Pacific. However, this railroad was far inland, no closer than sixteen miles to Bellingham Bay.

Probably undercapitalized, Canfield suggested to Cornwall that the B.B. & B.C. and the B.B.R. & N. should join forces, but Cornwall refused. Frustrated by the continuing failures to secure a rail terminus for Bellingham, prominent citizens offered to the first railroad reaching Bellingham Bay from across the North Cascades a whopping bonus equivalent to twenty-five percent of the assessed valuation of the four towns that made up Bellingham.

The winter of 1887–88 was so severe that little railroad work could be done. On December 15, 1887, the temperature sank to six below zero, which froze to the sand an experimental oyster bed *on salt water.* When a high tide came in, the whole block of ice, oysters and all, floated out to sea. As spring came, Canfield's B.B.R. & N. received word that the New Westminster & Southern would build a road south from Canada to connect with its line. Meanwhile, Cornwall quietly laid rails toward Sumas. In the fall of 1888 two locomotives arrived on the ship *Germania* for the B.B. & B.C., even though the line only had a few miles of track, mostly between Whatcom and Fairhaven at opposite sides of Bellingham Bay. It was said that, whenever a steamer came into port, the two locomotives, D. O. Mills and Black Diamond, huffed up and down to give the impression that Bellingham was an important commercial center.

That same fall two new figures appeared in the railroad saga — C. X. Larrabee, financier, and Nelson Bennett, who operated the Cokedale coal mines near Sedro Woolley. Bennett required access to a seaport and, together with Larrabee, proposed to build a railroad to the Fairhaven area if residents would donate certain lands. They likewise proposed to construct wharves, coal bunkers, a sawmill, and a good hotel. Dirty Dan Harris, who had become a major landowner and

influential citizen of Fairhaven, persuaded his fellow land-
owners to grant such concessions on the theory that remaining lands would rise sharply in value from the developments.
The demands were granted, and J. H. Stenger also sold his
Washington Colony mill site, water power installation, and
the wharf for a reported $42,000. Bennett and Larrabee's cor-
poration thus acquired major holdings in Fairhaven, as well
as 160 acres near Lake Whatcom and 110 near Lake Padden,
and started construction of the Fairhaven & Southern Railroad.

The following year Bennett bought Canfield's B.B.R. & N.
interests, thus acquiring rail rights from Skagit to Canada; in
1890 he made connections with the Seattle & Montana Railway Company near Burlington and then sold the whole combine to the Great Northern Railway. With the weight of that
giant company behind it, the missing links between the
Skagit and Blaine were filled in and on February 14, 1891, a
golden spike was driven at the international border at Blaine
to unite the lines and thereby provide continuous rail service
from Seattle to Vancouver. A celebration was held at the border with visiting dignitaries, Lieutenant Governor Laughton
of Washington and Governor Nelson of British Columbia.
Wild enthusiasm swept Bellingham, for residents assumed
that the headquarters of the Great Northern would be theirs;
before the year was out, dismayed citizens learned that the
offices were moving to Seattle. Bellingham had lost its
chance, once more, to become the first-class rail-seaport it so
fervently desired to be.

As a sort of consolation prize, Bellingham did become the
chief terminus of a transcontinental line when the Canadian
Pacific joined with the B.B. & B.C. Railway at Sumas. The
tumultuous celebration that marked the event in Bellingham
almost dissolved the new international relationship. As a
"super-spectacular" attraction, the fire companies from
Sehome and Whatcom lined up on opposite sides of the track
to greet the first train, which was supposed to arrive beneath
an arch of water played by the two hose companies. The
waiting firemen could not resist the possibilities of the situation and started a grand water fight. With bands playing

loudly the train slipped unnoticed right into the middle of the water fight. Jets of water from the powerful hoses broke coach windows and drenched the V.I.P.s aboard. They were good sports, fortunately, and all was forgiven. Damp but smiling, the dignitaries proceeded to the formal banquet.

Further difficulties arose. A large wooden arch had been erected across the tracks in honor of the event, from which the flags of the United States and Canada were displayed. Noticing that the British flag was hoisted slightly above the United States flag, a well-meaning youth climbed the pole to adjust them and, in the process, dropped the British standard to the ground. Insulted Canadians protested all the way to the halls of government in both countries.

Along with the land speculation encouraged by the railroad growth, had come genuine industrial expansion along Bellingham Bay. In 1887 the first fruit cannery opened and by 1888 the lumber business was moving ahead strongly. There were six big mills in the county — the Dellinger, Mills & Co.; Bowman Mill; Bellingham Bay Lumber and Manufacturing Company; Fairhaven Mill; Stenger Mill; Martin & Wyman Mill; and in 1889, P. B. Cornwall completed a seventh mill employing 200 men. The World's Fair Board heard of Whatcom County's famous logs and W. L. Davidson, commissioner for the State of Washington, came to select special logs for exhibition at the Chicago World's Fair. The sample logs were between sixty and a hundred and twenty-five feet long and twenty-one to forty-six inches in diameter.

When railroad routes finally had been established, the day of reckoning came for land speculators. Too often property had been sold to complete strangers, who bought with low down payments and poor credit references. Profits were spent before they were realized and, when the lull in land-buying came, those living on credit or paper wealth were in trouble. Creditors were unable to locate debtors, many of whom had moved on to new and more promising arenas. To add to the woes of local commerce, the entire nation faltered during the panic of 1893, which also brought Okanogan gold mines to a standstill.

First to waver were the banks, some of which had sprung

up like toadstools in the ferment of business speculation during the eighties. Officials of the First National Bank and of the Loan & Trust Bank were indicted for fraudulent banking, and angry crowds attended the trials, only to see them break down in a morass of legal complications. The extent of city and county graft was discovered to be extensive, but not much could be done about it. Little cash could be found in anyone's pockets, and men returned to the bountiful land for food. It became a period for barter, and a remarkable man named Charles Cissna hatched an idea that amounted to a local monetary system. He issued merchandise scrip in exchange for products of the farms and some factories; this was paper notes about half the size of regular dollar bills, which recipients used to buy supplies at Cissna's Fair Store. The merchant then sold the raw products in his own store or at wholesale to other parts of the country.

7

The Cascade Wagon Road Fiasco

The gold rush that had started in 1879 and faltered in the 1880s never really ceased; its character simply changed during the last decade of the century. Instead of individuals who washed out placer gold with crude equipment, mining was tackled by well-heeled, organized companies who brought machinery and industrial know-how into the mountains. But few mines were successful; the jumbled geology of the mountains defeated even the most experienced mining company. One would discover a rich vein, spend thousands on development, enjoy handsome assays, and then have the vein disappear suddenly; no one could predict where it might recur. Mining in the North Cascades was like picking buckshot out of a cougar's hide — a little here, a little there, with constant resistance. Even when gold was found, it was almost impossible to remove to a smelter. The North Cascades Highway was seventy-five years too late for the gold miners; the cross-mountain railroad never materialized.

For the ranchers of the Methow and Okanogan, too, the biggest problem was getting their cattle to market. Before the railroad was built to Wenatchee in 1892, cattle had to be driven to Ellensburg over country where forage was sparse and the terrain killing. Rustlers like the Black Shirts, who declared they only rustled cattle from the "big outfits who wouldn't miss 'em," added to the hazards of long drives.

Separated by the mountain range but united by their common problem of obtaining a road or railroad, Okanogan and

Stevens counties joined Whatcom and Skagit counties to put pressure on the State for help. With typical poor timing, the State of Washington took notice of the problem in the middle of the depression of 1893, when local governments were almost penniless. It established District Number One of the Road Commission for the North Cascades and appropriated the sum of $20,000 to build a wagon road, with funds requested from the counties of: Whatcom, $5,000; Stevens, $1,000; and Okanogan, $1,000. Because the route was presumed to go east to Okanogan County through Whatcom County, no money was requested from Skagit. With the $20,000 the legislature expected the commissioners to build a road from Bellingham Bay to Marcus on the Columbia River, specifying that it was to go near the Ruby Creek gold fields. That meant building 200 miles of road over some of the most rugged country on earth at a cost of $135 per mile. Okanogan County had no money at all, and the state treasurer refused to accept interest-bearing warrants for their $1,000 matching funds. County workmen accepted the warrants, for times were hard; suppliers of tools and materials would not. Whatcom and Stevens counties did manage to scrape up their funds. Without waiting for route approval, Okanogan County enlisted volunteer labor and soon built a passable wagon trail from the Methow Valley to 6,000-foot Twisp Pass, holding a maximum grade of 16 per cent with no switchbacks. Whatcom County roadbuilders concentrated on getting a route past Mount Baker to Ruby Creek; if the two work crews had been successful in getting over the mountains, the segments would *not* have met.

The legislature had appointed a three-man road commission to oversee the development of the Cascade Wagon Road: John J. Cryderman, T. F. Hannegan, and a Mr. Oliver. Before the commission let clearing contracts, it appointed a survey party to lay out a route. With enough supplies to last them one month, Banning Austin, E. P. Chace, H. Hall, and R. Lyle left Bellingham in May, 1893. They took a route different from Austin's previous trip, on an old Nooksack Indian path toward Mount Baker, but eventually found Austin Pass again and continued past Chain Lakes to explore the pass at the head of Wells Creek. Other than enjoying a spectacular view of Mount Baker, the side trip was fruitless because Wells was even higher than Austin Pass.

The men then set out along Ruth Creek. After a stiff climb the men came out into a gentle valley that pointed east, where gentle meadows made traveling easy. Whatcom County pioneer, P. J. Jeffcott, in his book, *Chechacho and Sourdough*, recounts graphically Austin's first glimpse of Ruth Creek Valley:

> To the right across the valley and creek arose the beetling crags of Ruth Range, whose sparsely timbered broken cliffs and spots of green showed tiny moving specks of white, the forms of many mountain goats. . . . To the east the glistening snows and perpetual glaciers of Ruth Mountain bared her frigid shoulders skyward to more than six thousand feet and formed the right hand gatepost to the pass. . . . On the left rose, grim and gray, the perpendicular walls of Granite Mountain, whose non-accessible heights stood like a huge stonecutter's monument.

According to the survey party's instruments, Ruth Pass was about 5,000 feet high, and from the summit there was range upon range of mountains to the east, with shadowy forms of valleys appearing between. Although they could not imagine just how a road would be built through the jumbled country, the explorers considered the pass to be the best way to cross the first big range. Given the choice of a name, R. M. Lyle, a truly devoted employee, declined the honor of naming the pass after himself and christened it after his boss — Hannegan Pass.

The party pressed on to Whatcom Pass, again at 5,000 feet and from there they could see the canyons of Little Beaver Creek and Big Beaver Creek, which led to the Skagit River. The Austin-Lyle party returned home to report that it was feasible to build a road to the Ruby Creek diggings via Hannegan Pass, and work started without delay. A contract for brush clearing was let at a cost of fifty-seven dollars per mile, surely a modest figure. Nevertheless, at the State Road Commission there was strife about the routing and charges of inflated prices for the clearing, of graft, and sectionalism. By the time twenty miles of crude right-of-way had been cleared to a point within two miles of Hannegan Pass, all work was ordered stopped late in 1893. Commissioners Hannegan and Oliver resigned from the commission, replaced by J. J. Donovan of Bellingham and E. M. Wilson.

As both Cryderman and Donovan were professional engineers with experience on large construction projects, the two men went on a brief inspection trip of the route in 1894 and returned to assert that the roadway could be completed with the balance of appropriated money — $15,000. It seems a strange recommendation from such knowledgeable engineers, when one realizes that the road still had to cross most of the North Cascades. The matter was further puzzling because, later in July, 1894, the two men went back to the mountains near Mount Baker to review the proposed route. At the same time, with no publicity, the Road Commission also sent Bert Huntoon and a companion identified only as Harry in a diary left by Huntoon, to explore the south fork of the Nooksack and take survey sightings.

A week after the two men had entered the mountains from the Skagit Valley, they were in seven feet of snow at Baker Pass, near the foot of Mount Baker. In 1868 Tennant and Coleman had failed twice before attaining Mount Baker in a carefully planned expedition. On July 13, 1894, Huntoon and his companion climbed the mountain in one morning just to see the view. They crossed the big glacier on the mountain's south slope and came to the volcanic crater that is below the summit. In his diary Huntoon noted that the crater was about 800 feet wide and at the bottom, about 400 feet below, a sulphur spring emitted hot fumes. Mount Baker continues to emit steam — sometimes heavily — to this day.

Huntoon climbed on to the summit in another two hours, commenting that it was a steep, hazardous climb with hands and feet in soft snow; that the route went along large cracks in the glaciers. From the pinnacle Huntoon took pictures, then descended to his camp.

A few days later Bert Huntoon and Harry built a raft and went up into the Baker River above Baker Lake, but the trip was cut short. When Bert was disembarking from the raft, he lost his balance and his pack swung around and hit his right knee. A hand pick fastened to the outside of the pack was driven into his kneecap to the bone. Despite the pain he insisted he would continue, but his knee soon became so swollen that he could not bend it. Returning to the cabin of trapper Bion H. Chadwick on Baker Lake, Huntoon sent Harry up the river to explore while he recuperated. Chadwick, a bear trapper, had rendered out gallons of bear oil; he smeared the evil-smelling stuff on Bert's infected knee and the old mountain remedy killed the growing infection. After a few days Harry returned to report there was no pass under 5,000 feet between the Baker and Skagit rivers and the survey was abandoned. When Huntoon was able to travel again, he and Harry ascended Swift Creek to Austin Pass and joined Donovan and Cryderman where they were camped near Nooksack Falls, ten miles west of Mount Baker, returning to Bellingham with them. Cryderman and Donovan then recommended to the State that the entire project of a wagon road over Hannegan Pass be scrapped because the passes were too high and the grades too steep.

Miners in the upper Skagit and businessmen in Bellingham reacted angrily to this recommendation, and P. B. Cornwall stoutly offered to pay half the cost of finishing the road himself. Banning Austin denounced Donovan and Cryderman's findings and defended his report that the route was feasible, while Wells, who had also explored Mount Baker, supported Austin. Because Donovan and Cryderman constituted a majority of the three-man commission, their position was obviously unassailable. Donovan hastened to Olympia to ask the legislature to spend the remaining appropriation instead to locate the cross-mountain road east through the Skagit Valley.

While the legislature was considering this request, nature was wreaking havoc in the Methow Valley, destroying the valley road which would connect to the proposed Cascade Wagon Road. Unseasonably warm weather in the mountains melted a heavy snowpack rapidly and, combined with cloudbursts, soon sent creeks and rivers over their banks. The swollen Methow River swept through the valley, washing out all the bridges built by the pioneer settlers. On May 31, 1894, mailman Ulrich Fries splashed knee-deep on his horse through the river on his trip between Pateros and Winthrop. The following day, the river, always swift but usually shallow and narrow, was a raging torrent and the horse had to swim. Fries described it in his book:

> There were many pine and fir trees, some three or four feet thick next to the roots, with the roots themselves sticking from five to ten feet in the air. There was no sign that the limbs had been broken. It looked as if some giant demon, or other unnatural being had taken them by the tops and thrown them into the swift, deep river to be carried away.

When Fries went up the valley, the river was undercutting the foundation of the hotel at Silver, the little mining town near Twisp, leaving its gable end hanging three feet into space over the water. Within two days the river had eaten away the ground upon which the town rested and store, hotel, saloon and other buildings collapsed. Silver was not rebuilt, and all that remains of the town today is a historical sign.

At Pateros the bridge washed out, leaving the Methow Valley isolated from the towns to the south, which were also inundated. Where the Columbia crosses the international border the river was fifty-six feet above normal level; and the abnormally swift current caused a ferry at Brewster to break its moorings and head for the Methow Rapids. With the help of a couple of brave men in small boats, the ferry's crew forced the boat onto a small sand bar near Pateros before it was sucked into swifter water. Hundreds of miles downstream at Portland, residents rowed boats into the railroad station, hoping to escape the flood by train.

There were odd benefits from the big flood in the Okanogan country. Layers of silt washed out of the mountains made the farmland more productive. The mosquitoes that had plagued the Okanogan River towns never returned in any quantity after the flood. Hordes of ants and mice that had plagued the settlers nearly disappeared and never again were numerous. A riverboat captain, William Groggins, took advantage of the extremely high level of the Methow River to deliver heavy mining machinery directly to the town of Methow, ten miles from the Columbia.

Despite the demands upon its meager funds for emergency road repairs, in 1895 the State made a further appropriation for a cross-mountain road, indicating that $4,000 should be set aside for the construction of a road to join Bellingham to the Skagit Valley, and that the Cascade Wagon Road should extend from Marblemount to Twisp. Eventually, the wagon road was to be thrust farther east to Colville and Spokane, and another $6,000 was appropriated for that purpose — 150 additional miles over three mountain passes and across two big rivers.

The appropriation of $4,000 for a connection from Bellingham to Skagit pleased the Bellingham, but not the Skagit merchants. Because the towns along Bellingham Bay were bigger and more prosperous than those in Skagit, the merchants feared that too much business would go to Bellingham. When asked to contribute $6,000 in matching funds, the Skagit County Commissioners were hostile; they simply took no action on the proposal, and the road could not be started. Delegations from Bellingham went before the commissioners to plead for compliance, and Bellingham businessmen and private citizens raised $1,000 to donate, if only Skagit would approve the appropriation. After intense pressure by the State, Skagit did make the money available in 1896; and a trail appeared out of the rocky ground along Bellingham Bay, a twisting thirty-five-mile route between the bay towns and Skagit.

With the Cascade Wagon Road on the schedule, the State Road Commission again sent a survey crew into the upper Skagit canyons to assess the situation. They found the trail to Ruby Creek, built piecemeal and with threadbare financing, to be rudimentary. It was not possible to get a horse all the way through the Gorge, because of the section known as the Goat Trail, involving ladders over rocks; but even as the survey party came into the mountains, Skagit citizens were taking steps to improve the trail so that pack horses could get through. Citizens donated their time for pick and shovel work. The ladies of Anacortes gave fund raising dinners and came up with $500 to buy blasting powder. Albert Zabel, who ran the Hamilton-Marblemount stage and a saloon in Hamilton, donated his stagecoach for transportation of powder, supplies and workers.

Blasting a trail out of the overhanging rock near Devil's Corner was treacherous. One day, during a lunch break, a man named Jackson went back to the rubble to look for gold ore in the newly blasted rock. The loosened rock above thundered down the cliff, taking Jackson to the bed of the Skagit River and burying him under tons of rubble. When the road was finished it was still only about six feet wide — just enough to permit a packhorse to get through without the pack catching on the wall. With a true flair for understatement, the State Road Commission commented that the trail was "picturesque and shows the energy displayed by the active interests of the Slate Creek mining district in opening a way of ingress and egress."

Pioneer Glee Davis, still alive and active at this writing, said that bringing in a Sibley stove over the trail was his biggest problem as a packer. A Sibley stove was an inverted funnel-shaped affair about five feet in diameter at the base, which rested on the ground in a cabin or tent. It had a door slightly off the ground and held a great deal of wood. The stove could be smashed down more or less flat for shipment, at least for a few times; and Davis tried to bring one over the Gorge Trail on a horse. Coming through one part of the trail where there was a considerable overhang, the horse and stove got stuck.

"Well, she started r'aring around," said Davis about his horse, "and I grabbed her by the halter and held her so she wouldn't throw herself overboard, while I unpacked the stove with the other hand. It all turned out OK."

After an exhausting two months of climbing around in the rugged upper Skagit to survey possible routes, the commission's survey party discarded the Gorge as a route, noting the difficulty of building even a narrow horse trail. They settled upon the Cascade Pass route, which followed Red Fox's old Indian trail almost exactly, from Marblemount to Twisp.

Work started in the spring of 1896. M. E. Field of Stehekin was given the contract for constructing bunkhouses to house the crews along lower Bridge Creek. He also acted as supplier for the crews, transporting materials from Lake Chelan. After deducting seventy-five cents for room and board, the average road crew member made less than one dollar and seventy-five cents daily.

In its later report to the State legislature the Road Commission apologetically stated:

> Owing to the limited appropriation and the great distance of road to be built the Board had to keep closest scrutiny upon expenditures . . . Only four feet of the road bed could be graded where heavy excavation was necessary. But the Board . . . made brush and timber cuts from sixteen to twenty feet in width and removed rock and stumps from the roadway; thus making *practically a wagon road* [author's italics] width except on rock barriers and steep side hills.

During the summer the road up the Cascade River was worked into shape about six miles toward the pass; and in 1897 another six miles to Gilbert Landre's cabin was roughed out, but *that is as far as the wagon road ever went.* From there on, remaining funds were used to improve the pack trail over Cascade Pass. Work terminated on both sides of the mountains, and the route officially appeared on State maps as State Highway #1 or the Cascade Wagon Road. The fact is that it never was a wagon road and no wagon ever went over it. From the Gilbert Landre cabin to Twisp Pass, the trail was in the category of "practically a wagon road except." This discrepancy did not seem to bother the State or its map makers, who perhaps did not know the true state of affairs.

Before the year was out, the flood of 1897 took out most of the newly completed construction work along the Cascade River; nevertheless, the *Chelan Leader* reported in 1897 that "An Olympia dispatch says the Cascade division of the state wagon road from Marcus to Marblemount is completed, leaving $7,400 of the $20,000 appropriated . . . to finish up the road in Stevens County."

In 1899 the State repaired some of the bridges in the Methow damaged by the flood of 1894 and also built twelve and one-half miles of narrow road between Lake Chelan and Bridge Creek. One wonders if the State's representatives ever did come into the wilderness; that year officials again declared "the wagon road provides a continuous highway for the movement of troops in case of necessity and particularly in protection of the northern frontier." To demonstrate the extent of improvement, George Rouse, a Methow miner, rode horseback from the mouth of the Twisp River to the summit of Cascade Pass, fifty-three miles in one day and a few hours — half the previous time required. However, this was one horse, not a regiment.

Six years later, Joseph M. Snow, the first State Highway Commissioner, visited the site of the Cascade Wagon Road and determined the true state of affairs, reporting that almost all of the money appropriated to that time for a road had been wasted.

8

The Counties Battle While the Mines Suffer

The battle over the connecting link between Bellingham and Skagit County was far from over; as soon as pressure from the State eased, Skagit County stopped raising money for maintenance and the trail deteriorated. The excuse was that hard times made expenditures impossible. However, depression-poor merchants were refinanced by 1899 when the Klondike gold rush ensued, and prospectors rolled through the Pacific Northwest once again, leaving cash in the tills of suppliers from San Francisco to Bellingham. So, when the Skagit County Commissioners sang the same song about lack of funds, the notes came out flat; clearly they planned to scuttle Whatcom County business as much as possible. When the Seattle and Montana Railroad, later the Great Northern, offered in 1901 to buy the right-of-way used by the road in Skagit County, the commissioners accepted — even though this cut the only existing north-south road between Bellingham and points south. The railroad paid Skagit County $8,000 "in excess of all expenses which would be incurred in the relocation and reopening of said road," and made an estimate of such costs. The commissioners deposited these sums in the bank and turned a deaf ear to any specific plans for immediate relocation of the road. They didn't say they wouldn't build, but procrastinated endlessly. Through political machinations and stalling, they managed to postpone re-linking the two counties for almost twenty years.

Lack of north-south road connections to other West Coast cities was particularly frustrating to Whatcom County. The Northwest corner was enjoying its own small gold rush at Mount Baker, where rich strikes were made at nearby Twin Lakes, starting in 1897. At least two of the mines — the Lone Jack Mine and the Boundary Red Mountain Gold Mine — paid off as much as one million dollars each. A sort of island, with the international border to the north, the impenetrable North Cascades on the east, and no road to the south, Whatcom County commerce was restricted to movement by rail and water.

One of Skagit County's excuses for not rebuilding the road promptly was that the commissioners felt the route along Bellingham Bay was impractical; that possibly was valid, but the State offered financial assistance in relocating the road. State law required, however, that a county must invest matching funds to obtain State funds; this Skagit County refused to do.

In 1903 the State legislature passed a law creating a State Highway Commission independent of control by the governors (which had been a problem), but the current governor, McBride, was from Skagit County and vetoed the law. Two years later the legislature prevailed and one of the first actions of the new Státe Highway Director was to offer $5,500 to Skagit County, requesting them to add the sum to their still-banked fund from the Seattle & Montana, and build the connecting road to Whatcom County. Skagit still stalled on the basis of locating an alternate route.

Supplying the mines of the upper Skagit was the plum that caused contention between the counties. A turn-of-the-century revival of mining there had stimulated supply business in the Skagit Valley, and money was being realized by some mining companies. Unless Whatcom County could gain access to the diggings — many of them within its own boundaries — through Skagit County, it was shut entirely out of the supply trade.

In 1906 the Ruby Creek Mining Company set up an ambitious project to mine the gravel near Ruby and the Skagit River, spending more than $300,000 on their camp alone. They completed a bunkhouse, cook shack, a small sawmill to provide wood for a four-mile flume, and built a complete hydraulic plant. Everything had to be transported by pack train, including the nozzle for the hydraulic plant, which was mounted on a block of cast iron. The company realized only $3,000 in gold, one per cent of its development cost. The buildings were abandoned, later to be used for a roadhouse known as Ruby Creek Inn. Luckier was Charles D. Lane, founder of the Eureka Mine on Slate Creek, who took out $150,000, enough to provide him with a lovely home and gracious living in his home city of San Francisco. For a time placer diggings on Granite Creek yielded fifty dollars a day per man. The Granite Gold Mining Company successfully worked the claims of George Holmes, the only known black miner in the North Cascades, a man who was a lifelong friend of John McMillan.

One of the biggest developments in the Slate Creek area was the Chancellor Mine, which constructed a power plant in 1906 at Slate and Canyon creeks. Later an engineer for Seattle City Light, Nicholai Aall built the plant and supervised the building of a sawmill, powerhouse, and a flume two miles long to a 240-horsepower generator that would supply power to the Chancellor and the Bonita mines. The generator, four feet in diameter, was hauled in over Hart's Pass and was cast in two semicircular sections for hauling; even so, it was a killing load for the horses. The Chancellor proved unprofitable and closed in 1907, leaving the remains of the equipment rusting away in disintegrating buildings.

While it lasted, the mining activity brought enough people over the Skagit Gorge Trail to justify a few crude hotels, like the inn of the Pressentins at Marblemount and the Outpost operated by the Davis family near Skagit Gorge. Little more than a shack, the Outpost carried basic provisions and offered crude overnight accommodations. In 1897 the Davis family (consisting of Mrs. Davis, a divorcee; Glee, age thirteen; and his brother, twenty-one) took over an old miner's cabin with four bunks and built a second small cabin near the trail to use as a roadhouse and hotel. Glee Davis recalls that they offered bed and board only, and that meals were forty cents and beds were twenty cents. After about ten years Davis built a bigger hotel with eleven rooms near today's Diablo Lake, then known as Cedar Bar. There was only a horse trail along the north side of the Skagit River past his hotel toward Ruby Creek, and it was impossible to use canoes above that point because of the rapids. The Davises kept a canoe at Cedar Bar to transport travelers bound for Thunder Creek across the river. For a time the remote hostelry did a brisk business.

Among the permanent settlers of the upper Skagit was Tommy Rowland, who settled on Beaver Creek to raise hay and to hire out as a packer. He named his homestead New Jerusalem and called himself the Prophet Elisha, berating visitors with heated religious doctrines and earning himself the reputation of being a nut. Glee Davis denied that, saying he was just eccentric, and liked to lead people on.

Eccentric — yes, one of Rowland's schemes was to engage a deep-sea diver to explore the bottom of some deep pools on Ruby Creek, where he maintained gold nuggets were lying. Contacting a firm on the Sound, Rowland hired a diver named Benjamin, who came with his equipment and made one dive only to find the "nuggets" were just shiny rocks.

The mines near Thunder Creek were extracting more silver than gold, and one of the most successful for a brief period was the Skagit Queen. Incorporated in 1905 for one million dollars, with twenty-nine separate lodes, the Skagit Queen constructed a large camp: bunkhouse, cookhouses, a storehouse and powder house, barn, and geological laboratory. All of the material, including a thirty-inch Pelton wheel and generator for power, had to go over the Skagit Gorge trail; and the company maintained its own pack string of forty animals at Marblemount. When the mine needed a heavy block for its compressor, and there was no way to divide the block for shipping, the packer selected one of the biggest mules and put the block on its back. Because the mule couldn't tolerate the weight for more than a few minutes, the packer built a tripod and hoist; and every few hundred feet he stopped, hooked the block onto the tripod, and lifted it off the mule's back to give him some relief.

The many switchbacks on the narrow trail also made long objects a problem; Glee Davis refused to try to take a twenty-foot single section of rail to the mine. Packer Jerome Martin packed in big coils of cable by putting one coil on the lead horse, then running a length back as far as the next horse in line to add a second coil, and so on to the next. One can only shudder at the incredible tangle if even one horse had bolted.

The Skagit Queen investors were excited by assays of as much as $672 per ton but could not know that veins only went into the mountains a short way. To acquire more speculators, the firm's publicity department embarked on a full-scale stock promotion, with offices in Seattle, Tacoma, and distant Lowell, Massachusetts, touting the stock. When the mine sank into financial ruin five years later, the investors were left with gold dust only in their imaginations. The British Mining Company acquired the claim, but they too failed.

Other mines in the Thunder Creek area included Bornite, Willis Everett, Standard Reduction, Colonial; but only a few ever made money. During this intense flurry of activity the miners bitterly condemned both counties and the State for their inability to provide adequate trails or to finish the Cascade Wagon Road. Not only was the Bellingham-to-Skagit portion in contention, but also the point on the upper Skagit River where the two counties met. Skagit was reluctant to build its road because completion would increase Whatcom County's tax rolls from the mining properties, and Whatcom dragged its feet because supply business would go to the closer Skagit towns. The miners became so irked that they developed a movement to form a new county out of eastern Whatcom and Skagit counties, so they could make their own improvements.

The voice of the mining community was heard, faintly, in 1905, when on January 27 a bill was introduced in the State legislature proposing $25,000 for a road from Marblemount to a point near Mill Creek (Slate Creek area) and, wonder of wonders, both Whatcom and Skagit representatives worked for its passage. The bill passed on March 9 without opposition, providing $24,000 for survey, construction, and maintenance of such a road, plus a section from the mouth of the Methow River to Barron, which would provide a cross-mountain connection. It was stipulated that Whatcom should contribute $8,000 and Skagit $5,000. In May, Whatcom County informed Skagit that it would suspend its cooperation unless Skagit also built the long-obstructed road along Bellingham Bay. The exasperated State government took legal action against both counties to force them to spend the appropriated funds and do the work required.

When nothing much had been accomplished a year later, State Highway Commissioner J. M. Snow demanded that Skagit County build its connecting road to Bellingham and, unless it did spend the money received from the railroad "for relocating and reopening said road," the State would sue them. Unruffled, the commissioners said, in effect, "Go ahead, sue!" The matter went to court, Skagit County won, and the stalemate continued. In 1907 the legislature amended its road policies and no longer required counties to provide matching funds, but if a county wanted help from the State for any State roads within its borders, it had to ask for such funds. Skagit County did not ask, because such a request would have brought the State's insistence that they build the connection; so two years later the State decided to build without the county's consent and brought in convict labor from Walla Walla to construct roadbed. The legislature also appropriated a small sum for the Cascade Wagon Road again, but the State Commission and many Skagit citizens were so opposed to the concept at the time that they refused to spend the money. Even the *Concrete Herald*, later a strong proponent of the North Cascades Highway, in 1913 stated that the cross-mountain road should be abandoned and the money spent closer to population centers.

Although the convicts hacked out and graded three-quarters of a mile of road along the cliffs near the Whatcom-Skagit border on Bellingham Bay, the fickle State legislature in 1911 overthrew the entire State highway law and made no appropriations for roads, so brush reclaimed the work done. The road between the two counties was not completed until 1920 — twenty-five turbulent years after it was started. Not until 1919 and into the next decade did anything further occur about the desire for a cross-mountain road.

9

The Birth of Okanogan and Omak

Today the North Cascades Highway ends at Omak, but in 1893 when the legislature appropriated money for a wagon road to Marcus, Omak and Okanogan did not exist. Only a few ranchers occupied the benchlands there. Like the Methow Valley, the area west of the Okanogan River was part of the Chief Moses Reservation. When it was opened for white settlers in 1886, first to appear was Dr. Joseph I. Pogue to homestead on a barren flat above the river and practice medicine. An unusual pioneer, Dr. Pogue was a medical doctor, educated at Northwestern University, Evanston, Illinois. He had spent ten years in successful medical practice in Iowa, but was lured west by the open frontier life. Recognizing the potential of the dry land if the magic ingredient of water were added, Pogue installed the first irrigation system in the county and planted an orchard of apple and prune trees. Although he ranged far and wide over sparsely populated ranch land to treat the sick, he gleaned more income from his orchard and from breaking horses to sell to the ranchers and miners.

Just a few miles south at the junction of the Chilliwhist and Okanogan rivers, L. C. and Mary Malott settled in 1886, even though their son was drowned in the river on the day of their arrival. Because Malott's farm lay at a busy wagon road junction, it became a logical stage stop, and he built an immense barn that held forty horses and a roomy home in which he served meals to travelers at twenty-five cents a person. He invested in 250 head of cattle in 1889 but, like many others, he did not expect severe winters and had not put up hay; so the sudden snow and ravaging Arctic cold that blew across the open mesas in 1892 destroyed his herd and he saved only 35 of the 250 by feeding them flour and potatoes. Discouraged by this attempt at ranching, Malott noted Pogue's success and decided to plant fruit trees. Within a few years he was producing enough fruit to take wagon loads to the Republic gold camps of north central Washington.

Despite the occasionally severe winters, the lush grasslands did spawn cattle ranches. Among the big spreads were those of Hiram "Okanogan" Smith near the Canadian border, and of Robert French in the Scotch Creek Valley; French later became a State senator and Smith a representative. The ranchers fought the traditional problems depicted in western movies — drought, snow, rustlers, sheepmen. Prior to 1900 the cattlemen had exclusive use of the range, but in 1901 Frank Clerf brought 30,000 sheep onto Okanogan County ranges and other smaller operators herded in another 20,000. Clerf found trouble immediately. First burning 700 tons of Clerf's hay, unknown arsonists then sent unsigned notes enclosing matches to ranchers who raised and sold hay, mute warning of what would happen to them if they sold hay to sheepmen. In 1903 the arsonists burned another 200 tons of Clerf's hay. One C. C. Curtiss bought cattleman Charles Guthrie's ranch near Okanogan, not revealing that he intended to run sheep, and later brought in a big flock. When sheep grazed off his land and onto that of cattlemen, Curtiss was told firmly to keep his sheep confined — or else. But there were no fences, and the animals continued to occasionally wander. One night a group of unidentified men entered Curtiss's corral and slaughtered hundreds of sheep, silently beating them to death with clubs and axes. The sickening butchery was not discovered by the sheepman until the next morning, and no one came forward to apprehend the culprits.

Horse raising was both a necessity and a popular hobby. Some ranchers imported fancy thoroughbreds and Hambletonian trotters to use as Sunday horses or for racing, a mania ranchers shared with their Indian neighbors, the Colville and Nez Perce to the east. A unique race was won by a pinto horse owned by G. B. Clark of Brewster, making national headlines. Four hundred western stockmen raised a purse of $20,000 as a publicity scheme to demonstrate the stamina of western-bred horses and five horsemen left Olympia on May 1, 1912, to visit the capital of every state in the union. The first to return — Pinto — won the prize. Inevitably there was widespread horse thievery, and horses with Okanogan brands showed up as far away as Montana and western Washington. Around 1925 a man named Frank Willis and his son-in-law drove almost a hundred horses over the old Cascade Pass Trail in early fall and sold them in Skagit and Whatcom counties. This incredible feat went unapplauded because ownership of some of the horses was disputed. Some were wild, unbranded horses but others — who could tell? Willis was convicted for horse theft and put in prison. However, stray horses were a real problem; only those with brands could be identified positively and others were always in contention. In December, 1920, the sheriff of Omak rounded up a bunch that were roaming the streets of town and sold them at prices ranging from twenty-five cents to eight dollars apiece, and later disposed of unclaimed horses.

A little town called Pogue had grown up around the orchards of the doctor by 1906, and nearby there was a hamlet called Alma; concluding that Pogue was too difficult a name for a town because strangers might call it Pogyou, the two settlements joined under the neutral name of Okanogan in October, 1907. Typical of western towns, the first transaction of the new government was to grant a saloon license to the Big Dan Saloon. The Okanogan Hotel existed, and the rest of the town was little more than a few unpainted buildings of rough construction; the streets were trails that straggled through the sagebrush and rocks.

One winter twenty of the new settlers decided to hold a dance in Keene Hall. Most had come from the Midwest, where respectable citizens wouldn't be seen at a public dance hall, so organizers of the dance, Harry J. Kerr, Paul Nelson, and A. M. Storch sent out formal invitations. Unfortunately, the new town had arrivals every day and some of them didn't get invited. Furthermore, the saloon crowd that hung out at Joe McDonald's Saloon resented their exclusion and declared that this "highbrow" stuff was no good and that they were going to shoot up the dance. On the night of Okanogan's big social event two armed men were placed at the entrance to the hall and the participants danced all night because they were afraid to go home until dawn.

On June 17, 1902, through the work of Senator Newlands of Arizona and Congressman Wesley D. Jones of Yakima, with the support of President Theodore Roosevelt and Gifford Pinchot, Congress passed the U.S. Reclamation Act as an indication of its concern for public lands. Through the petition of the newly formed Okanogan County Improvement Club, the Okanogan Irrigation Project became one of the first projects tackled by the Reclamation Service. Three thousand miles away in Washington, D.C., few employees of the Department of Interior knew where Okanogan was, much less anything about its geology. The first man sent to select a dam site for the Irrigation Project, a Mr. Noble, had practical experience only in selecting lighthouse locations along the Alaskan Coast. Noble explored the eastern slope of the North Cascades and decided on a site near Conconully, a sound enough decision, but the dam he built there would not hold water. Noble was recalled and the department sent Christian Anderson, a man who previously had made a survey of land above the Okanogan River. Instead of using broken rock and cement like Noble, Anderson put down a plank barrier and used water under pressure to wash fine silt off the hills to pack the dam. Conconully Dam was completed and dedicated in 1910 and remains today, having been reinforced several times. When the irrigation ditches were completed, a ditch rider on horseback opened the weirs for individual ranches so that each got its proper allotment.

With keen interest developing in irrigated fruit orchards, in 1909 a Bostonian named Mears moved into Malott with the grandiose vision of himself as lord of the manor. Operating as the Boston-Okanogan Apple Company, he bought 700 acres above the town of Malott and set out fruit trees. Mears planned a great mansion overlooking the valley, from which he would control a massive irrigation system operated by automation. After stripping thousands of dollars from outside investors who became interested in his scheme, he disappeared leaving only a huge completed basement (still on the property) and the trees. The orchard continued long after Mears left with his profits.

A short distance north of Okanogan, 300,000 apple trees were set out on lands irrigated by the Okanogan Project, and there the town of Omak was incorporated in 1911. Within two years the Great Northern Railroad laid its tracks into Omak to tap the sharply growing fruit-packing industry. The fame of Okanogan fruit spread, when Dr. Pogue routinely won prizes with his fruit at fairs and expositions; and in 1915 winesap apples grown at Fred Conklin's orchards near Brewster won the Sweepstakes Prize at the San Francisco Exposition.

Politics in frontier towns was often a no-holds-barred affair; the 1914 county election was no exception. By this time Conconully, the county seat, was remote and in an economic decline, so both Omak and Okanogan declared that they would fight to win the county seat. To support their contention that Okanogan was a town populated with roughnecks of no refinement, Omak supporters gave voters a picture of a drunk hanging over the hitching rail on First Avenue in Okanogan. Okanogan retaliated by producing a trick photograph that made it appear that the railroad terminal between the two towns was much closer to Okanogan than to Omak. When Conconully accused Okanogan of not having enough money to build a courthouse, even if it won the election, a group of autos left Okanogan for Conconully on August 4 carrying twelve heavily armed men with their revolvers and shotguns showing prominently. At Conconully the men dumped out a canvas sack containing $12,000 (with photographers handily there to record the event) as proof that Okanogan did have such funds. Thereafter postcards of the picture were made up and sent to all the voters. Alarmed by the prospect of all the publicity luring bank robbers to his town, the county treasurer at Conconully implored the Okanogan men to take their money back to Okanogan. Harry J. Kerr, president of the First

National Bank, privately agreed to do so but aloud said loftily: "No, we don't want it. There's plenty more where that came from!"

Later that night Kerr and a companion went to the rear of Conconully's bank and received the money, quietly returning it to Okanogan. Three weeks later Omak deposited $12,000 in currency at Conconully, but the also-ran publicity fell flat.

In order to gain the support of Methow Valley citizens who were agitating for separation into a new county, Okanogan citizens published a signed letter indicating that they favored such a new county, but specified boundary lines that they knew would never be accepted. When election day dawned, Omak made its campaigners vote before going out to drive voters to the polls, but Okanogan decided those few votes wouldn't matter and got its men into the country early in the morning. By the time Omak men got on the scene, most citizens had already voted and been influenced by Okanogan drivers. Okanogan won the election, and W. C. Gresham of Conconully is reported to have sent this message to Kerr: "Come and get your damn county seat!"

Omak could have been vindictive toward Okanogan but, led by Bob Wright, chairman of the County Commissioners, it showed good sportsmanship and supported its archrival Okanogan. It could afford to be tolerant; most of the new industry was locating in Omak and producing sharp growth for that city. Accelerating its growth was the designation of Omak as the official point from which homesteaders could claim land, when the 400,000 acres of the Colville Reservation bought from the Indians was thrown open for settlement in 1916. The same year a frost-free warehouse provided central packing facilities for the fruit growers next to the railroad siding.

Omak's preoccupation with horses continues on into today. Starting in 1920 the stores conceived the idea of a monthly Market Day carnival with drawings for prizes. To attract further crowds of shoppers, races through the streets were held, participated in by both whites and Indians, and rodeos featuring such formidable bucking horses as Two-Jump Louie challenged the courage of local cowboys. These informal merchant-sponsored events were the forerunners of the world-famous Omak Stampede, an annual event which draws at least half of its contestants from the nation's top rodeo circuit. Evolving from the wild cross-country races of the Indians, who sometimes raced their horses twelve miles, the Suicide Race, an event held during the Stampede, where contestants plunge down a cliff into the Okanogan River, was immortalized in Walt Disney's movie, *Run, Appaloosa, Run*.

10

Roads and Rails
in the Methow Valley

Until the designation of a new state highway to be built
along the Methow River from Pateros to Hart's Pass in 1905
(a designation resulting from the work of Methow legislator
W. A. Bolinger), traffic up the valley went over the ragged
hills above the river. Freighting wagons required six horses
and were built off the ground to accommodate the deeply
rutted roads, had elevated seats for the drivers, and covers for
the freight-carrying portion. Supporting the wagon were
heavy wheels with wide iron tires, on which there were
brakes to control speed on downhill slopes and to hold the
wagon on uphill grades when the team had to stop and
"blow." The freighters took pride in their teams, currying
them to a shine and brushing out their manes, tails, and heavy
fetlocks. The harness was sturdy and bells were mounted on
the steel frames. These served to warn oncoming freighters in
time for one of the wagons to turn out to avoid a confrontation
on some narrow part of road. Isolated ranch families also
found the bells a cheerful link with the outside world.

Along with the freight, passengers jolted up the valley on
the crude roads. Blossom Hanks, a young teacher in the valley in 1904, described her trip from Brewster to Twisp:

The boat landing at Brewster had been washed away and passengers from the boat landed on the bank where the wharf had
been. The steward, stepping off first, stirred up a rat-

tlesnake. . . . After disposing of the snake . . . we all rode up to the hotel in a wagon. Tracey Heath, stage driver, loaded on my trunk. I understand that we traveled the Brewster Mountain Road as no through road had been built up the Methow at that time. It was a long pull up the mountain. Tracey was entertaining; had a good voice for singing, and then told us stories of the wild country into which we were going. Once, when we stopped to breathe the horses, he got a bottle . . . and offered his passengers refreshment. Neither of us accepted, however, and Tracey put the bottle back . . . not without taking a nip himself.

The teacher went on in her letter to a friend to say that the passengers were fed at Halfway House, where a change of drivers and horses also took place,

. . . the driver being now an older man whose face was hidden by a luxuriant growth of whiskers and who was called Preacher Davis. Toward evening we had a glimpse into the Methow Valley.

Strung across suitably narrow places in the river were flimsy bridges made of split logs nailed together or of heavy planking. Such structures were known as low-water bridges, and most of them washed out every year during flood season. Although built above flood waters, the later steel-supported bridges had poor engineering, if any; the approaches frequently washed out, and wooden floors on bridges would often catch fire. These tenuous structures were an adventure to cross; signs warned travelers never to cross the bridges at faster than a walk, to avoid setting up fatal oscillations. Violators were fined twenty dollars in court. The rampaging flood of 1948 washed these bridges away, too, leaving only the modern concrete ones to span the river.

After Bolinger's bill was passed, a survey crew went into Hart's Pass in October, 1905, but was driven out by an early snow, and had to work at the Pateros end of the route. During the same sudden snowy period, the caretaker of the Eureka Mine, William B. Robinson, set out for Mazama at the foot of Hart's Pass to get his mail and supplies. That early in the season, Robinson did not have his snow goggles with him and when it snowed, followed by brilliant sun, he became totally snowblind. Alone on a precarious mountain trail, temporarily blind, he could not hope that anyone would come along until spring. He had no choice but to feel his way along. Robinson could detect the ruts made by wagons, and he traveled along the ridge in between; he knew also there was a precipice beside him and could hear the Methow River rumbling far below. Later he said that he fell down time after time, and

> ... needed a walking stick to feel my way. Finally I found one, part of a downed tree, but couldn't break it off. I grew colder and was chilled but couldn't move fast enough to keep warm. I was about to quit when I heard a different sound to the water. It was Lost Creek coming into the Methow, and I knew I could make it.

Representative Bolinger continued to monitor the progress of the Methow Valley road, and in 1906 and 1907 crews completed more than half of the seventy-five miles from Pateros to Winthrop and picked up the project after new appropriations in 1909, completing a road to Hart's Pass. The spartan funds were stretched by using convict labor, which cost about sixty cents a day, one third the cost of private labor. Although a minimum-security camp was required to handle the convicts, the prisoners were allowed to work in regular clothing — a small concession that seemed to give them greater self-respect, many of them working so well that they were later paroled. In fact, the prisoners and local people finished the road late in the year because appropriations ran out and local citizens contributed labor and funds.

It was no freeway, this Pateros-Hart's Pass Road, but freighters found it an improvement over the hill climbing. In 1915 Leonard Therriault, a man who later was very influential in obtaining the North Cascades Highway, went into the freighting business between Pateros and Winthrop. Therriault's brother Paul operated from Pateros, Leonard from Twisp. On a typical day, using horse-drawn wagons, Leonard and a helper left Twisp or Winthrop laden with butter from the creamery, maybe a few head of hogs, furniture for someone who was moving, a bit of gold from a mine, and a passenger or two. They arrived at Gold Creek for the night, where there was a "noon station" or stage stop — just a big barn and house where the horses and men were fed and bedded down for the night (the men usually slept in the haymow). The next day the rig proceeded down to Pateros, unloaded and reloaded, returned to Gold Creek and Twisp — a four-day round trip.

When the Therriault brothers started their freight run, a competitor had the mail contract, but in 1916 they were awarded the privilege and bought a four-horse hack for mail. In summer they used a Model-T Ford for the passengers and in winter a sleigh, as the roads were not plowed in those days. During the winter of 1916 Leonard got the idea of adapting a Model-T to run in the packed-down sled tracks by cutting about eleven inches off the axles to make the car as narrow as a sled. This custom car was used for passengers all one winter successfully. The following year the company bought a one and one-half ton Velie truck, and in 1918 two one-ton trucks with wide, solid tires welded onto the rims. If one ran over any sharp object, he would lose a chunk out of such a tire and thereafter it would go thunkety-thunk with every revolution. When the tires became unbearably noisy, the whole wheel had to be sent to Wenatchee for repair. Between Methow and Carlton there was a clay hillside which, when wet, was as slippery as if greased; during spring the freight truck had to leave Twisp about three A.M. to cross this area before it thawed out.

Even though the freighters hauled gold occasionally through the half-settled valley, there never was a robbery. One time though, Therriault arrived at the noon station and was met by the distraught wife of the stationmaster, who told him that her husband had just taken strychnine because he was jealous of her. Leonard rushed into the house and, perfectly calm, there sat the husband waiting to die. Leonard called the doctor at Twisp, then rushed out to get a neighbor to help him hold down the man, who refused to take an emetic. The husky stationmaster threw both would-be rescuers aside and managed to avoid help. Soon the effect of the poison began to take its terrible toll, and the helpless people had to watch the man die horribly.

Concurrent with the development of the Pateros-to-Hart's Pass Road, there were daily announcements about railroads that supposedly would "cross the mountains any day now."

Shortly after 1900, Cryderman of Bellingham made another of his surveys for the B.B. & B.C. Railroad, startling the Methow Valley citizens with news of a possible railroad from Bellingham to Spokane. J. J. Donovan periodically spoke to groups in the Methow and was quoted in newspapers, assuring the residents that the route selected was practical and that things would happen any moment. First he said the road would cross from Deming to Slate Creek, then that it would go via the Skagit Valley. There was a rumor, hotly denied, that the Union Pacific was behind B.B. & B.C. Another rumor was that the Canadian Pacific was going to build from Spokane to Sumas, connecting there with B.B. & B.C. Great Northern was supposed to have crews in the valley doing surveys for a road from Rockport to Spokane. H. E. Marble's editorial in the *Methow Valley News* of October, 1905, succinctly summed up the cynicism:

> By actual count there are now twenty-seven railroads proposed to be built through the Methow Valley. We have been keeping count of them and speak in authority. It is liable to take up every ranch in the county in furnishing rights of way and terminal grounds. There will be nothing left for the rancher to do but to pack his grub box and hit for the tall hills to avoid being run over by the cars.

Less sarcastically, he wrote again the following year that the chief difficulty, as always, was the failure of various parties to locate a feasible pass through the mountains. Other lines were in the mountains by 1909 — the Chicago, Milwaukee and St. Paul Railway and the Skagit, Cascade and Chelan Railway Company. Two electric railway companies proposed to run lines through the mountains but never specified how they were going to do it: the Okanogan Electric Railway Company proposed a line up the Twisp River all the way to Seattle, and the Bellingham, Mount Baker & Spokane Interurban Railway from Deming to Spokane. In 1911 Methow Valley citizens, skeptical that any of the schemes would hatch, formed the Methow Valley & Washington Northern to build a railroad simply from Pateros to Winthrop. Although wide support was given to this proposal, nothing ever came of it. Methow Valley remains railless to the present day.

11

The Skagit Valley Hums

Even though the rails never crossed the North Cascades, the building of a railroad to the upper Skagit Valley in 1908 triggered the explosion of Skagit's logging business. The Puget Sound & Baker Railway Company was a joint venture by logging men, including: L. T. Dempsey, J. J. Dempsey, W. C. Butler, E. G. English, and Fred E. Pope. Small spurs were built to serve logging camps and to transport logs to the mills; and when the railroad prospered, it added a subsidiary, Washington Tugboat Company, to move logs by water in 1913. The floating stock included tugs that became familiar to every person along the river — *Black Prince* and *T. C. Reed* — as well as several scows and small craft. From live trees to Puget Sound booms the combine controlled the transportation of logs.

Instead of casual farmer-loggers who cut shingle bolts in their spare time, there were now well-capitalized big companies in the woods. In December, 1904, the *Mount Vernon Argus* reported that there were 115 firms employing 4,005 men in saw and shingle mills in Skagit County, and another 166 firms employing 4,317 men in Whatcom. Vast timberlands belonged to Ed English and his variously-named companies, to the Dempseys, to Hamilton Timber Company (forerunner of Scott Paper Company), Sound Timber Company, and others. To process the logs, enormous mills developed, not only at Hamilton and Sedro Woolley, but also in small communities like Clear Lake and Big Lake.

Unlike today's loggers, who live in the towns and commute to the woods each day, the early logging men usually lived in camps in the hills. Most were single and were drifters, working for a few months at one camp and then moving on. Often groups of men wandered the logging camp circuit as a unit, with a leader who bargained for the whole crew. Because it was a hard, dangerous, and lonely life, like that of early cowboys, the loggers spent their time off in carousing, fighting, patronizing the red-light districts, and, of course, drinking. In the early part of the century, Hamilton had sixteen saloons, Concrete about twenty, and Sedro Woolley literally dozens; indeed, the latter — as center for logging, mining, and railroading — was a very tough town. It was customary to shut down logging in the woods only twice a year, usually around the Fourth of July — when the companies repaired their equipment — and for Christmas.

The average logger came into town with a paycheck of $400 or $500 (a logger made two to three dollars a day) ready to "shoot the works." First he bought the clothes he needed for the coming six months: heavy black underwear, cork shoes, stag shirts, wool socks, and a jacket. To make sure he could get back to camp, he bought a railroad ticket. Along with a couple of bottles of whiskey, he put the clothes and ticket in a suitcase and left it in the care of the attendant at the local railroad depot. Then he strutted back to town to blow the rest of his cash. Sometimes a man would simply hole up in one tavern or cathouse and give the proprietor all of his money — telling him to advise when it ran out.

Some old-time residents defended the loggers' attitudes by pointing out that the men were all single transients and had to let off steam somehow; that the madams of the town were really very nice people in many ways. One well-known operator of a brothel was frequently seen carrying baskets of food to the hungry in town, a paragon of virtue on the one hand and of questionable morals on the other. In later years, the red-light district succumbed — not so much to the law as to the rivalry among establishments. The most well-known "house" in town, the Fern Room, was entered during the day and vandalized by a member of a rival house. The furniture was slashed, stove wrecked, lamps smashed, but curiously, the precious big mirrors were not touched.

Some of the loggers sought the bright lights of a bigger city like Seattle and usually wound up on the waterfront. At the loggers' hiring hall in Seattle, Archie McDougall ran an informal loan service for the broke logger, who could borrow only enough money for a ticket back to his job in the Skagit Valley. The Skagit logging firms worked with McDougall and repaid him for such desperation loans.

While at work in camp, the loggers were as proper and gentlemanly as men anywhere. The *Skagit Valley Herald*'s charming, elderly columnist of past days, Molly Dowdle of Hamilton, was a flunky at the age of fifteen, waiting on tables in the Lyman Timber Company camp. She was not to talk to the loggers at all, except concerning food orders. Despite the segregation demanded by the management between the few women and the loggers, the girls sometimes played practical jokes. Molly related how two male cooks who lived next door played poker with their cronies until late hours of the night, keeping them awake. One afternoon when the cooks were away, the girls crawled up on the roof and stuffed a gunny sack into the stovepipe of the cooks' bunkhouse. Shortly after supper, one of the cooks went to the cabin and built a fire so it would be warm when his friends came to play cards; instead of merely creating a smoke cloud, the plugged-up chimney caught fire. A bucket brigade quickly put out the fire, and because the incriminating sack burned, too, no one but Molly and her girlfriend ever knew how that chimney fire started. The only damage to the cabin was a hole around the pipe.

A few of the loggers were married; one was cursed with an extremely jealous wife. Suspecting that her husband was fooling around with one of the flunkies, the wife sneaked up to the logging camp after dark to spy on him. Shrill and unmistakably feminine screams aroused the relaxing camp members that evening, for the unfortunate wife had stumbled into a knee-deep pool of diesel oil behind the bunkhouses, oil that had been drained out of the locomotives. Rescued by the flunkies, the disgraced spouse was put into a hot shower, clothed in makeshift but clean garments, and sent home on the speeder (a small "people" car on a railroad) along with her thoroughly embarrassed husband.

Although the camps were very isolated, there was little opportunity for crime; after all, most holdup men were not interested in tackling a camp full of tough loggers. Nevertheless, in October, 1908, the boss — Ed English — was kidnapped while driving home from the Tyee Logging Company's camp about five miles south of Mount Vernon. The kidnappers commanded English to write a note to his wife, asking her to place $5,000 in gold coins in a designated spot or English's ears would be cut off. One man went to town to deliver the note while the others waited with English in a secluded woods. Although he was chained to a tree and threatened with death if he attempted to escape, in the darkness English found a loose link in the chain, got his hands free, and crawled away — then ran to a nearby home and telephoned his wife. She called the sheriff, who arrived just in time to nab the man delivering the note, but he was merely a messenger hired in Mount Vernon and had no connection with the gang. By the time a posse arrived at the woods where the gang had been waiting, all had fled and were never caught.

Forest fires raged uncontrollably each summer, as they had for centuries, usually touched off by electrical storms in the summer-dry woods. In the Mount Baker National Forest between 1920 and 1930 alone, there were seven fires that burned 50,300 acres of timber. The biggest share of this was from the Big Beaver Creek fire of 1926, which started from lightning and burned all summer until the rains came, leveling 40,000 acres near Ross Lake.

A wild conflagration burst out in May, 1912, on the Dempsey Logging Company property and, according to the *Mount Vernon Argus*, 30,000 acres burned in two hours. The fire had been smoldering near Birdsview for several days, when a high wind came up on May 14 about noon, creating a fire storm with a roar heard six miles away. With unbelievable speed the fire swept forward, killing five Dempsey men — all that remained of one were his scorched cork boots and his belt buckle. One man at the Dempsey camp climbed into the water tank while the fire blazed through; still he burned his face and hands because he had to hang onto the side of the tank to avoid falling into the water.

Families living in the woods were caught by surprise and fled for their lives. Mrs. W. P. Parker, cook at the English bolt camp, ran through the brush five miles to safety. Also in the path of the fire was Molly Dowdle's family. Molly's mother had given birth to a baby only the day before. Leading a horse for his mother to ride, Molly's older brother carried her smaller sister and Molly cradled the new baby in her apron as she ran through the trackless woods, crying — not because of the fire — but because she had new patent shoes with red buttons, which she had to leave behind.

There was no escape by rail, because the trestles burned, too. Risking the collapse of the structure and loss of his own life to save the equipment, one intrepid engineer roared across a flaming trestle with his logging locomotive. When the disaster ended, four logging camps had been destroyed — two of Dempsey's, two of English's — plus acres of prime timber.

From the depressed logging areas of North Carolina and Kentucky in the early 1900s came the Tarheels, men who brought their families and culture with them and whose descendants are among the finest Skagit families today. These were not drifting loggers, but family men who lived in the woods near the camps, worked during the day and went home to their rough cabins at night. Hard-working, family-loving, and fiercely independent, these mountain men influenced the attitudes that prevailed in Skagit County, where citizens honored those who took care of themselves. Along with their self-sufficiency and spotless cabins, their homemade sausages and hams, the Tarheels brought with them another custom that caused trouble — the traditional mountain moonshine still. "White lightning" bubbled away in the back barn of many a remote farm, most of it consumed by the man's family and friends; but during prohibition, a few sold their alcoholic products to big-city runners. Cock-fighting, also frowned upon by the law, flourished in clandestine meetings in the backwoods.

Growing and changing like an amoeba to pace the developing logging industry, a remarkable little Sedro Woolley firm was gaining a foothold in the manufacturing of equipment — Skagit Steel Company, absorbed in 1969 by the Bendix Corporation. Originally, the firm was called the Sedro Woolley Iron Works, a shop of 13,000 square feet built in 1901 as the only foundry north of Seattle, by John Anderson, John Fritsch, Reuben Fowler, and John Henderson. The firm said its work force consisted of nine men and one horse. A couple of years after its founding, David McIntyre came to work as a mechanic and by 1922 had purchased a controlling interest in the company.

Because logging was a relatively new industry, solutions to problems of log-handling were approached with completely open minds. The steel company's first contribution to efficiency was a unique stump puller that required only one man and a horse.

When Sid McIntyre, David's son and a graduate engineer, joined the firm in 1921, he was able to solve an unusual problem with a product that swept the logging industry. Bloedel-Donovan at its Alger operation wanted to clear a small millpond of dead cedar logs and, because existing logging equipment was steam driven and very large, they had no suitable machinery to do the job. At the time the Ford Motor Company was advertising its Fordson tractor as a power source, suggesting that one could jack up the wheels, put a belt on the tractor wheels, and use it to run machinery. McIntyre developed a versatile little log hoist or logging donkey from this concept and, even though the local loggers laughed at the idea of gas-driven logging machinery, he formed a marketing company within the Skagit Steel Company and sold the device as the "Little Tugger." It sold so well that soon Skagit Valley Ford dealers were scouring the Northwest to locate enough Fordson tractors to meet the demand for Tuggers. Back in Detroit, sales executives looked at sales figures from little Skagit County and could not imagine what such a small territory was doing with so many tractors. To satisfy his curiosity, Henry Ford himself came to Sedro Woolley in 1924 to see the Skagit factory.

Because of the versatility of the gas-driven hoist, loggers

began to hook them up in succession, or parallel — as many as four tractors or a "quad" — to provide power for bigger, heavier jobs. In response to this need Skagit Steel commissioned the Buda Engine Company to develop a new type of high-torque, low-speed engine to run a more powerful log hoist. Because of their successes in this field, the firm was given a contract for building the first construction hoist on the Columbia River Project in 1924. Still another innovative development by Skagit Steel, the Ruxtel axle, resulted in the firm's conversion of Ford cars into Ford trucks *before* Ford Motor Company manufactured trucks.

There seemed to be no limit to the adaptations of Ford products for purposes never dreamed of by the manufacturers. In order to get logs off steep hills, Skagit laid down ordinary peeled logs as tracks out of the woods; removing the big wheels of the Fordson tractor and replacing them with larger wheels which had a wide groove in the middle, the company adapted the tractors to use the log tracks as a guide. Little cars were added behind to make a sort of Tinkertoy railroad — the only catch was that the pull had to be downhill. This unique tractor was made obsolete by the invention of tractors with continuous treads by such companies as Caterpillar.

As logging cleared the Skagit Valley, farming became big business. In 1906 the Carnation Milk Company built a condensed milk plant in Burlington, which employed 200 men; in 1908 the Mount Vernon Condensed Milk Company added a tin can manufacturing company; and Fisher Rolled Oats constructed a mill in the same area. Local farmers experimented with unusual crops. Some, such as Holland bulb growing, and berry cultivation of every kind, became mainstays of modern agriculture. Although floods periodically inundated the flat deltas in the western Skagit, destruction was offset by the fertile silt deposited over the land, stretching like a green platter from Sedro Woolley westward.

In 1909 a warm wind blew for three days, melting the snow in the mountains and, combined with heavy rains, the Skagit River poured over its banks on a rampage from Rockport to the Sound. Dikes crumbled like children's sandcastles, undermined barns fell on valuable livestock, and farmers were trapped in their homes. The Indians were the heroes of this disaster, rescuing countless stranded people in their big canoes. Other serious floods occurred every few years, not to be controlled until the building of dams on the upper Skagit.

The land was bountiful in another unusual way. The area around Concrete, thirty miles upriver from Sedro Woolley, abounded in a special clay and limestone used for the making of cement. Pioneer Amasa ("Pegleg") Everett was responsible for calling this deposit to the attention of New York investors during a trip to the East; and in 1906 the Washington Portland Cement Company was organized to develop the materials. Organizers of the company were: J. C. Eden, Captain E. E. Caine, Jacob Furth, Michael Earles, W. P. Holfus, William Piggott, and James Hedge, with Eden appointed as the active manager. At first, Washington Portland used a flume about five miles long, several feet wide, and thirty feet off the ground in places, to bring water to their cement plant from Lake Shannon. Because it repeatedly washed out during high water, the company replaced the flume with a steam plant nearer the cement works. Pioneer Concrete resident, Gordon McGovern, recalls that, years later, he and friends took saddle horses to the upper end of the old flume and galloped them down the broad, still sound structure.

Since the rock quarry lay higher than the site of the cement plant, Washington Portland built an incline railroad to haul rock; as one car went down laden with rock, it pulled an empty car up for a new load. The firm constructed a tram directly from the quarry to the plant; a later owner, Superior Portland Cement Company, built an extension of the tram but, on occasion, cables broke and the cars ran wildly down and fell into the lake. The job that established the importance of Concrete's industry was a contract to supply cement for the Lake Washington canal in Seattle. In 1914 the United States government bought a vast quantity of cement for the Pearl Harbor drydock in the Hawaiian Islands; and during construction of Grand Coulee Dam, cars left every half hour from Superior's Concrete operation.

For a time, two firms operated at opposite ends of today's

Concrete — Washington Portland and Superior Portland; in 1918 the latter bought the former. The merger was not without some bitterness. Gordon McGovern worked at Washington Portland during its last night shift, while a big party was going on downtown to celebrate the joining of the firms. He recalls that, whether by erroneous orders or by deliberate intent, a master switch was opened and electricity was shut off to the plant one-half hour before the shift was over, leaving the workers in darkness to grope their way out. There was cement in the workings and, before anyone could be found to restore power, all of it hardened and the new owners had to go in and chop it out.

In 1925 Puget Sound Power & Light Company started the installation of Lake Shannon Dam, also known as the Lower Baker Dam. Inevitably, the flooding of the country above the dam drove out some old homesteaders, including Mrs. Joe Glover, ex-wife of Concrete's sheriff. The power company reimbursed this lady by giving her a launch, which she and her sister operated commercially on Lake Shannon for many years, carrying passengers and freight to the upper reaches of the Baker River. When Mrs. Glover and Nell Wheelock weren't running the boat service, they operated a small telephone company, and it was not uncommon to find either of them on a pole doing line repairs. In their "spare" time these two extremely active women had a dance band that was highly in demand for Concrete parties.

Living above Baker Lake in the shadow of Mount Baker was Joe Morovits, who sometimes has been described as the hermit of Mount Baker. The role suited his behavior at first. No one knew where he came from, but he appeared in the Baker River area about 1916, clad as the other miners in rough clothes, saying little about his past. After installing a water system he ran a small aerial tram for hauling rock from two or three small claims to a stamp mill.

Like other frontiersmen, he worked hard and kept mostly to himself. Periodically he boarded the train for Seattle, ostensibly to restock supplies, but not returning for weeks. Imagine the surprise, then, of a Concrete resident who encountered Joe Morovits on a Seattle street — all but unrecognizable in a fancy suit, broadcloth shirt, a beaver hat, and sporting a fashionable handlebar mustache. Curious, the resident made inquiries and found that Joe was well-known and well-liked as a ladies' man and apparently wealthy businessman, although no one seemed to know the source of his funds.

Back in Concrete, Morovits declined to offer any explanation about his double life, continuing to mine his claims. Long after Joe Morovits had left the Northwest, during renovation of an old Seattle hotel, owners found a trunk in their storeroom that contained Morovits' clothes and papers that indicated he had been a mining promoter. The fine clothes and confident manner of the controversial miner might have been a front for a con game or — who knows — he may have taken significant gold from his claims.

More likely the hermit of Mount Baker was Buckskin Joe Eaton, who spent nine years alone on Bacon Creek. This taciturn man claimed, in the few times he ever talked to anyone, to be the brother of a United States Senator. Usually he passed hikers on the obscure trail near his cabin without a word. The grizzled old man wore buckskin fringed garments and a cartridge belt with an old rusty revolver strapped around him, the gun rusty and useless. He wouldn't allow animals around his cabin, much less humans, and lived on potatoes and vegetables that he raised. Although he was a squatter on government land, the Forest Service closed its eyes to his presence as a harmless old man. He died as alone as he had lived; a hiker's dog howling mournfully at his cabin door caused the animal's owner to investigate — Buckskin Joe had been dead about two weeks.

With so much activity and prosperity in the Skagit Valley during the first two decades of the century, no wonder criminals eyed it as ripe for harvesting. The year of 1914 was when robbery exploded. On February 20 three men held up the Great Northern train between Burlington and Bellingham in a daring, Jesse James-style heist. The robbers boarded the train at Burlington and, somewhere between there and Chuckanut Bay, they stepped out into the vestibule and donned masks. When they reentered the car, they told startled passengers, "Never mind, it's just a joke. . . ." But one

Chief Moses (shown with his wife) once controlled the area now known as the Methow Valley.
(Courtesy of Okanogan County Historical Association)

2. Captain Henry Roeder. (Whatcom Museum
Collection, Bellingham, Washington)

Fort Okanogan (artist's interpretation). From here Alexander Ross departed in July, 1814, to locate a
trail across the North Cascades. (Courtesy of Okanogan County Historical Association)

4. The B. B. & B. C. train arrives in Bellingham, 1891. (*Whatcom Museum Collection, Bellingha[m]*
Washington)

5. Part of the precarious trail to the gold fields of the Skagit lay over a bridge that hung from the walls of the Skagit Gorge at the Devil's Elbow. (*Whatcom Museum Collection, Bellingham, Washington*)

6. Giant Cedars, Whatcom and Skagit counties. (*Courtesy of Photo Collection, University of Washington Library*)

7. Glee Davis and his wife Hazel. Glee still lives in Sedro Woolley. (*Courtesy of Seattle City Light*)

8. Ruby Inn at Diablo Lake. (*Courtesy of Seattle City Light*)

9. Winthrop, 1896. (*Courtesy of Okanogan County Historical Association*)

10. Typical Okanogan homestead. (*Courtesy of Okanogan County Historical Association*)

11. Ruby City, a gold rush town. (*Courtesy of Okanogan County Historical Association*)

12. Mount Vernon, 1884. (*Courtesy of Skagit County Historical Museum*)

13. Harrison Clothier. (*Courtesy of Skagit County Historical Museum*)

14. Alex Barron, left, and Guy Waring. The men are sitting on one of the extra-narrow wagons developed to haul gold and supplies on the mining roads. (*Courtesy of Okanogan County Historical Association*)

15. Pogue orchards, 1886, forerunner of today's thriving fruit-growing industry in the Okanogan/Omak area. (*Courtesy of Okanogan County Historical Association*)

16. Conconully, about 1890. (*Courtesy of Okanogan County Historical Association*)

17. Early Omak; note raised sidewalks and buildings with false fronts. (*Courtesy of Okanogan County Historical Association*)

18. Equality Colony, 1900. (*Courtesy of Photo Collection, University of Washington Library. Photo by Peter Hegg*)

19. The Field Hotel, which now lies under the waters of Lake Chelan. (*Courtesy of Photo Collection, University of Washington Library*)

20. Logging in Skagit County. (*Courtesy of Skagit County Historical Museum*)

21. Logging camp. (*Courtesy of Skagit County Historical Museum*)

. Bellingham in 1910. Photo taken from today's State
d Holly streets. (*Whatcom Museum Collection, Bell-*
ham, Washington)

23. Ed Kikendall with one of his sled
dogs.

Hazard Ballard and his wife Zora at the Azurite Mine. (*Courtesy of Okanogan County Historical*
ociation)

25. Logging truck, about 1920. (*Courtesy of Photo Collection, University of Washington Library*)

26. Early freighting in Methow Valley; teams hitched in tandem. (*Courtesy of Okanogan County Historical Association*)

27. First Methow Valley trucks, 1914. (*Courtesy of Okanogan County Historical Association*)

In Okanogan, horse racing through the streets was encouraged by the merchants. (*Courtesy of nogan County Historical Association*)

29. Horse thieves and captor. (*Courtesy of Okanogan County Historical Association*)

30. Frank Matsura, center, Japanese-American photographer from Conconully and Okanogan with two unidentified friends. (*Courtesy of Okanogan County Historical Association*)

31. An early lookout's cabin. (*Courtesy of Okanogan National Forest*)

32. Sheepherder's camp. (*Courtesy of Okanogan National Forest*)

33. Francis Lufkin, father of the smokejumpers, Twisp, 1939. (*Courtesy of Okanogan National Forest*)

34. Seattle City Light excursion boat on Diablo Lake. (*Courtesy of Seattle City Light*)

35. The tug *Boundary* in Ross Lake. (*Courtesy of Seattle City Light*)

36. J. D. Ross. (*Courtesy of Seattle City Light*)

. Horseback trip leaves Ross Dam to travel the route of the proposed North Cascades Highway. (*Photo urtesy of* Wenatchee Daily World)

38. Former Washington Governor Dan Evans and Methow Valley pioneer Les Holloway officially op◄ North Cascades Highway, September, 1972. (*Photo courtesy of* Wenatchee Daily World)

39. Les Holloway and Da◄ Evans clasp hands to symbo◄ ically join the east and we◄ sections of the road at Rair◄ Pass, September 29, 196◄ (*Photo courtesy of* We◄ atchee Daily World)

stationed himself at the front of the car, the second at the rear, and, while one held a gun on the passengers, the other went through and asked for valuables. When the gunman turned to lock the door behind him, Thomas F. Wadsworth, a Canadian, jumped on the bandit and wrestled with him. H. R. Adkinson from Vancouver and R. L. Lee from Bremerton leaped to Wadsworth's assistance. When the gunman seemed to be losing, the second bandit strode up and coldly pumped bullets into all three would-be rescuers, killing them, then shot through the car at random to discourage further opposition. Someone in the train pulled the emergency cord, the train came to a screeching halt only a hundred feet from the Samish rail station, and waiting passengers could see into the lighted car, where everyone sat with his hands up. Several men started to enter the train, only to be met by the thieves who had guns drawn as they left; first they climbed into the tender of the engine, then changed their minds and fled into the darkness.

Shocked and angered by the wanton murders, the sheriff instituted a massive dragnet for the robbers, which went on for months. Rumors were followed up — that a strange gray launch had been cruising in the Bay before the robbery, that smoke had been seen on Cypress Island, that a bloodstained suit was found in Tacoma along with clippings about the holdup. In late March an ex-convict, George Ball, was arrested in Alberta and returned to Skagit County to face trial for the crime. Ball was later cleared of the crime, but had some nervous moments when he arrived with the deputy at Mount Vernon and was met by a crowd in a lynching mood because — by sheer chance — Ball came at the same moment as a deputy from the upper Skagit was bringing in a murderous bandit who had left a trail of blood behind him as the "True Love" bandit.

Charles Hopkins had been captured while he slept in the little town of Van Horn. His crime spree began in Seattle when he killed a man with a bed slat. Shortly thereafter, when arrested as a suspicious character in Everett, he shot a police officer and two others in cold blood. On the move again, he took to the woods and near Everett held up two laborers and changed clothes with one. Near Arlington he encountered three loggers walking down the railroad tracks, marched them down the tracks at gunpoint, and shot the three down. A survivor who played dead was able to identify the killer as the same man wanted in Seattle and Everett, because he had a curious set of tattoos across the backs of his eight fingers that read TRUE LOVE.

The alarm went out to the Skagit Valley, toward which the man seemed to be moving; and a few days later Hopkins appeared at Frank Yeager's farm near Van Horn, asking for a place to sleep and something to eat. One of Yeager's farmhands noticed the tattoos on the man's hands; playing it cool, he quietly told Yeager to get the man out of the house. Yeager suggested to Hopkins that he go to Van Horn, where H. C. Ely rented out a room behind his store; Hopkins complied, falling into an exhausted sleep at Ely's. Meanwhile, Sheriff Joe Glover had been alerted and moved in silently with his men; he was able to quietly enter the room and handcuff Hopkins before he awakened. When Glover brought the man toward Mount Vernon to the jail, he was mobbed in every town by those who wanted to see the infamous bandit. Thus, by the time Glover and the deputy who brought in Ball arrived, the crowd was in an ugly mood, but law prevailed.

Citizens had not stopped talking about these two affairs, when there was an audacious holdup of the Sedro Woolley bank in October. Bank personnel were expecting the possibility of robbery. They had seen strangers hanging around for more than a week. Therefore, when the robbery did occur just before nine o'clock on a busy Saturday evening, the cashier was armed; but this job was planned by professionals. Before the bank was entered, two of the gang created a disturbance on another street to draw attention away from the bank; then the others thrust their way to the cashier's cage. Cashier John Goodall fired at once and slightly wounded one robber but, as soon as his revolver was emptied, the bandits held him at gunpoint along with two other employees, while their companions swept money into a bag, then forced Goodall to open the safe. Meanwhile, the two on the side street shot up the town wildly, in an effort to scare everyone off; an unfortunate ten-year-old boy, standing more than a block away, was shot and killed.

As the thieves climbed into a getaway car, Fred Cardine opened fire, wounding one of the men but receiving a bullet in his own leg in return. For several days reports that the men had been seen here and there trickled in. Five days later, the setting of the saga shifted to the Blaine border, where the bandits held up a customs officer about two-fifteen A.M. and escaped into Canada. Sheriff E. A. Wells hastily organized a posse to pursue them; while he was gathering up his men, H. G. Keith, Great Northern special agent, and Clifford Adams, Canadian customs officer from White Rock, and Immigration Officer Burke set out northward along the Great Northern tracks, reasoning that the bandits would go that way. Moving fast, they caught up with the robbers. Hearing a noise in the bushes, the pursuers yelled, "Come out of there!" and were answered by the bark of five pistols. The three men returned the fire, and at a distance of perhaps thirty feet, the deadly duel went on in darkness. Burke's head was grazed by a bullet; and Clifford Adams fell mortally wounded. The fugitives retreated into the brush and Burke, who had only been dazed, picked himself up but could not find his companions. Believing himself the only survivor, he stumbled back down the tracks into the arms of Sheriff Wells and his posse. Wells took Burke back to Blaine for medical attention; and at dawn the posse found Keith still alive but Adams, as well as one of the robbers, dead. A quarter-mile away the posse found a second dead robber; and the nature of his wounds indicated that he had been severely wounded by the officers, had dragged himself for a short distance, then either shot himself through the head, or was shot by his friends. About $3,000 in cash was found on the first robber, $250 on the second.

The five bandits now had dwindled to three, and the Canadian provincial police took up the chase. The final act of the drama took place two days later at the Ferndale bridge, eight miles north of Bellingham. Alerted by farmers who had seen the thieves, Sheriff Ed Wells and his men laid a trap. An automobile headlamp was rigged up as a searchlight on the bridge, and five deputies were stationed there. About mid-night two fugitives approached the bridge stealthily; the blinding light went on in their faces, and one deputy yelled "Hands up!" When the two reached for their guns, they were shot dead. More of the money was recovered, but the fifth bandit remained at large. The men were identified later as Russian immigrants, and it was believed that the band was part of a well-organized larger group which had been robbing banks all over the Northwestern states.

With so much bloody crime occurring within a few months, Skagit residents were understandably jittery; the valley had been a relatively peaceful place. Possibly one has to sympathize, then, with two young burglars who attempted to rob a Mrs. Thomas Bahr. When confronted in her home while she was ironing, the woman whirled around and whapped one of the burglars across the face with a hot flatiron! The men left.

XXXXXXXXXXXXXXXXXXXXXXXXXXX

12

The Forest Rangers

High in the mountains, a different kind of North Cascadian wandered the valleys and forests at the turn of the century — men dedicated to protecting the trees and the rivers, the fish and the wildlife, instead of searching for personal gain. These were the forest rangers, the hatchery superintendents, the firefighters, the trail builders. Undersupplied, underpaid, and underinstructed in what was expected of them — they used hard work and common sense to solve their problems in these early days of conservation.

In 1891, the Forest Reserve Act was passed by Congress, enabling the President of the United States to proclaim certain areas of the nation public lands. In February, 1897, the bulk of the North Cascades as presently included in the National Park, Forest, and Wilderness, was included in the Washington Forest Reserve under proclamation of Grover Cleveland. Jurisdiction first was given to the Secretary of the Interior, later was transferred to the Department of Agriculture, under Chief Forester Gifford Pinchot. Washington residents bitterly resented the removal of rich timberlands from private development and resented even more strongly regulation by a remote federal government run by easterners. The *Chelan Leader* reflected these sentiments in an editorial on March 5, 1897:

> Never, since the days when William the Conqueror laid waste the whole of the land . . . has such robbery of public territory been perpetrated as that which, by the late proclamation of

91

Grover Cleveland, alienates nearly eight million acres of public domain from the people of the state of Washington.

About a year earlier in 1896, the State moved to set up a hatchery program, proposing that the first hatchery be built on Baker Lake, as it was the only spawning grounds for sockeye salmon on the Sound. First to be built was a trap across the mouth of Baker Lake in seventy feet of water. Driven ten feet into the bottom, the pilings were left twenty feet above water level to provide anchoring points for a hanging webbed barrier. Pounding in one-hundred-foot pilings was no small task.

The heavy, steam-driven pile driver was cast in sections of about 250 pounds, so they could be packed eighteen miles on horseback to the site and assembled there. Tarred webbing weighted with chain was suspended from the piles to the bottom of the lake. In the center of the barrier, a small pen sixteen feet by twenty feet was constructed in such a way that milling salmon could enter but not escape. The air pump required for the divers, who checked underwater frequently for holes and fouling, was so heavy that it had to be brought into the camp suspended on a pole between two packhorses.

The fish traps were completed by the federal government, which bought the hatchery project in 1899; buildings for the crew were ready by 1903. That same year, Henry O'Malley, the young superintendent, left camp to marry and bring back his bride. When the newlyweds arrived, they found their home in flames. O'Malley's lieutenants had been cleaning up the yard and allowed a trash-burning fire to get out of control. O'Malley and his bride spent their honeymoon with the crew in a dormitory.

By 1905 the crew had completed a sawmill and planer, which enabled them to replace the original buildings. A generator was installed and telephone lines strung from a nearby Forest Ranger station. For a while, life was almost gentle; but in 1914 fire claimed the hatchery building and barn. Five years later, the rebuilt camp was leveled again, when — on a hot July afternoon with only the cook in camp — a spark jumped out of the stove and ignited the kitchen. The man fled from the building, still carrying a freshly baked cake. The blaze spread with such ferocity that everything — including the crew's personal gear — was lost. Because ten million fish eggs were in process in the tanks, the crew remained in the mountains living in tents and cooking over open fires in order to save them.

The construction of Baker Dam in 1924 severely interfered with the return of spawning salmon, until Puget Power installed a trap at the bottom of the dam and transferred the caught fish to Baker Lake in tank trucks — a practice they continue still.

Between 1905 and 1909, Pinchot's Forest Service employed a few men as Forest Guards. Their job was to build trails, watch for fires, and explore the territory assigned to them — thousands of square miles of wilderness that Weldon Heald vividly described in his book, *The Cascades*:

> . . . packed solidly with hundreds of square miles of soaring peaks massed together in lines, groups, and knots. They rise steeply thousands of feet from narrow valleys clothed in a jungle-like growth of huge evergreens and tangled underbrush. . . . Hundreds of glaciers mantle the summits, hang high in cirques under rocky ridges. . . . And hidden away among these twisted, convoluted mountains are enough lakes, meadows, waterfalls, alpine basins, and sweeping panoramas to keep the lover of the outdoors busy for a lifetime.

Into this wilderness came one of the first Forest Guards, C. C. McGuire, on May 1, 1909. He was given the princely sum of $300 to repair a sixteen-mile trail into Finney Creek from Sauk, which involved building a bridge across a canyon sixty feet wide where Gee Creek joins Finney. If he had any remaining funds, he was to continue building trails. With a package of beans and bacon, a badge, marking tools, and a "how-to-do-it" book, the young and enthusiastic McGuire trudged over a faint path to a log cabin on an abandoned homestead. He found the place already inhabited by hundreds of mice and immediately started building a frontier mousetrap.

Cutting the top from a five-gallon oilcan, he strung a wire across the opening through a small tin can opened at both ends and partly filled the oilcan with water. Baiting the trap by tying two pieces of bacon on the small can, he leaned a flat stick from the floor to the top of the large can and was ready for business. Within minutes a mouse ran up the stick and, not being able to reach the bait, jumped the few inches necessary onto the small can, which promptly rolled over and spilled him into the water. In his memoirs, which he left to the Mount Baker National Forest, McGuire commented:

> The war was on. . . . Twice that night I emptied the can of dead mice. My first count was 62 and at least as many more on the second count. . . . I spread my bedroll on the old bough bank and crawled in. In a few minutes mice were in bed with me; that I couldn't take so I moved outside. Mice were even nesting in my boots by morning.

After the restless night, McGuire hiked back to Sauk to backpack in the supplies he needed for the trail building, and to hire an assistant. Within four days he had built the bridge, cleared the old trail, and made three miles of new trail. With no fires to fight, he posted the forest boundary by tacking up with wooden pegs the required cloth signs and blazing trees to mark the limits.

In October, 1909, the Forest Service gave civil service examinations in Bellingham for the new post of Forest Ranger. Sixteen potential Rangers took the test, including McGuire. A far cry from modern requirements, here were the problems, according to the *Memoirs*:

> 1. From the foliage, identify ten species of trees grown on the Mt. Baker and give common and technical names. If you can spell the latter, more power to you.
> 2. Fall a tree ten or more inches in diameter with an axe. In giving this test a stake was driven in the ground about 20 feet from the tree. The victim was allowed to select the point where the stake was driven. All he had to do then was to fall the tree so that it would drive the stake further into the ground. His skill was determined by the nearness of the tree bole to the stake. Only three candidates out of the sixteen survived that test, one man actually driving the stake.
> 3. Figure magnetic declinations on the four quadrants of the compass. In those days it seems no one thought of the idea of setting off the compass dial.
> 4. Run and pace a triangle, prepare the field notes and compute the acreage.
> 5. Demonstrate your ability to use a seven-foot cross-cut saw.

6. Tell the boss man what ingredients and how much of each you would use in preparing a batch of biscuits.

7. How to build and put out a campfire.

8. Pack a horse. This was a toughy — the pack consisted of two loosely tied sacks of oats, an axe, a mattock, a shovel, and a cross-cut saw. Also five days supply of grub for one man — all unpacked — and a conglomeration of cooking equipment. Not only was your skill tested but you worked against time. Many would-be rangers fell by the wayside on this test. One bewildered candidate got the pack saddle on backwards with the britchen over the horse's head and used the breast strap for a double cinch. Next he picked up his lash rope and cinch and after he walked around the horse a couple of times he gave up in despair, remarking "there is no ring on this saddle that will fit the big hook on the end of this rope."

Only four survived the test: Ralph Hilligoss, Carl Bell, Grover Burch, and McGuire. New Ranger McGuire was assigned to Ruby Creek and given an axe, saw, and hammer (no money) to build himself a cabin. Enlisting the help of another Guard, McGuire dismantled an old shack at the head of a miner's flume, floating the boards three miles down the flume to the site of his proposed sixteen-by-eighteen-foot cabin.

While the two men were traveling out of the mountains for winter supplies, the snows caught them. At the Devil's Corner in the Skagit Gorge, the drip from overhanging rock had completely blocked the half tunnel with ice. They chopped through, and to prevent the pack horse from slipping over the cliff to its death, the two men tight-lined it across. One rope was tied to the horse's neck, another around its tail, and both were snubbed around trees on either side. While the man behind let out the rope, the one ahead took up the slack. In this way the horse was supported in the center of the rope. Although it fell to its knees several times, the animal regained its feet and made it across. By the time McGuire bought supplies and struggled back to his cabin, the snow lay seven feet deep.

The following year, McGuire was assigned to a cabin at Diablo Lake and given the supervision of a gigantic territory ranging from Hart's Pass to today's Ross Dam, and from Diablo Lake to Park Creek Pass. With two men he patrolled over rough and hazardous trails. On one trip into Diablo from

Marblemount, he had a new Kalamazoo cook stove and an old typewriter on a pack horse, plus horse feed, food, and blankets. The horse broke through a snow bridge over Gorge Creek and rolled down into the Skagit River, smashing the cook stove and skinning himself up. McGuire spent two hours building a makeshift trail to get the horse back on the Goat Trail.

In addition to patrolling the forests, the Rangers had to investigate land claims and supervise logging by private companies under contract. Homesteader claims in existence at the time of the Forest Reserve Act were recognized, but as time went by, they were contested, one by one, for not complying with the Homestead Act, namely, that the land be suitable for agriculture and be farmed with "due diligence." Any citizen could prospect for minerals on public lands. He staked a claim to prospect and filed it with the county *after* showing that he had done one hundred dollars worth of work or spent one hundred dollars on materials. If he proved that minerals existed, the claimant received patent of his claim.

In the early days such claims were seldom contested. Later, filings were examined by a geologist who determined if there were meaningful amounts of mineral before patent was granted. When a person held a patent, he could not be denied access to his claim; but the Forest Service had (and has) the right to dictate standards for access roads and, by mid-century, the right of minimizing environmental damage. In fact, the government did not have to permit access by road — just "access" — and when Kennecott Copper wanted to mine near Glacier Peak in 1967, the United States permitted only aerial access to the site. The dissolution of land claims proved to be a painful tangle and a source of hot contention by citizens.

As indicated, most of Washington's citizens were antagonistic to federal control of their lands, favoring instead State regulation. In August, 1910, Governor E. M. Hay, with the support of Governors Norris of Montana and Brady of Idaho, sternly rebuked conservation politicians at the National Conservation Congress in St. Paul:

I am as strong a conservationist as I can be. I am . . . convinced that the people of Washington are more competent to administer the reserve of Washington than any bureau in Washington, D.C. I am sorry to have to take issue with the former president [Theodore Roosevelt] . . . but I am for State conservation.

Governor Hay pointed out that vast amounts of land were removed from the tax rolls, contributing nothing to county and State expenses for that area. One month later at a conservation meeting in Spokane, Hay reemphasized his objections, saying bitterly:

Significantly, 95½% of Federal reserves are located in the Pacific Coast and Rocky Mountain States. The eastern States have had the use of their natural resources; they have dissipated them and now insist they have a right to participate in the resources of the western country. They maintain that the resources of the West should be conserved for all the people of the nation.

Rangers stationed in the Okanogan and Chelan areas not only had forests to monitor but sheep as well. Between 1910 and 1930, the open forests from Lake Chelan to the Canadian border were leased to sheepmen for grazing. About a dozen operators moved flocks, using herders and dogs, from the plateaus east of the Columbia to the high meadows of the North Cascades. During his two years (1918–19) as a Forest Guard (later a Ranger) on the Methow River District, Richard Grantham spent most of his time trailing the sheep herds. He counted them when they came off the ferries on the Columbia, then followed the flocks as they drifted over Billy Goat Mountain toward the upper valleys to make sure the herders kept them moving. If left to graze too slowly, they destroyed vegetation entirely, and conservation of grass was part of the Forest Service job. By the time the sheep got to the high country, it often was time to return. Then back they would come, their numbers swollen by the new lamb crop. Cattlemen did not always take kindly to the intrusion of sheep. On Skull and Crossbones Ridge, between Conconully and Loomis, cattlemen and sheepmen tangled in a range war that left wounds on both sides.

In Oregon, tick-infested sheep had spread their bugs to

wild animals, causing a terrible problem. To avoid this occurring in the Methow Valley, Forest Service personnel built
a dipping vat near Pateros by walling off a natural mudhole
with gates at both ends and filling it with lime and sulphur
sheep dip. A steam engine shot live steam into the water to
warm it. When the sheep came off the ferries, they were
herded into the pool and forced to swim to the opposite end.
Later, after being herded another eighteen miles to Gold
Creek, they were forced through a second vat of dip before
being permitted to continue.

A philosopher, Tom McArdle, sums up the Ranger of early
times, "The Ranger then was a doughty cuss, who chewed up
nails and spit out rust." Doughty or not, the Rangers did need
communication; by 1925 a bush telephone system had been
established along most forest trails. It consisted of a single
line that ran freely through periodic insulators fastened to the
trees. When a Ranger wanted to contact someone, he attached
a small receiver/transmitter unit to the line, thrust a stiff wire
into the earth to serve as ground, and rang up the person.
Ingeniously simple, the telephone worked beautifully. Furthermore, the free-running, slack line gave somewhat and did
not break if a tree fell across it.

Until radio communication became effective, bush or
crank-type telephones also connected the network of lookout
stations that perched atop strategic high peaks. Gene Lovejoy
of Omak, who was a lookout on 7,300-foot Baldy Mountain in
1943, said that the fire control office gave a special ring each
day, which all lookouts were supposed to answer. If any
watcher did not respond, someone was sent to investigate.

Before he was sent to his tower, a small room on tall scaffolding, the lookout was trained in the location of fires by
using compass bearings and maps, in radio operation, and
basic first aid. Most were young college students who were
willing to work all summer without relief for the one-hundred-
dollars-per-month salary paid in the 1940s (less food), enjoyed
the isolation, and returned year after year. Included in the network of stations were those on Sulphur Butte near Baker
Lake, Church Mountain and Dillard Point near Mount Baker,

Miner's Ridge in the Glacier Peak Wilderness, Monument 83 near the Canadian border in the Pasayten Wilderness, Goat Peak northeast of Mazama, Lookout Mountain southwest of Twisp, and others. Several of the stations still operate during times of extreme fire danger.

The lookout's day began at four-thirty A.M. and ended at dark — maybe. At dawn, when the forests were damp and quiet and storms unlikely, he hustled around to do his chores; thereafter, he sat in his tower, often reading, but looking up every few minutes to scan his assigned area, a panorama of dense forest punctuated by mountain peaks.

Because the station was in a cleared or burned-over area to provide visibility, it also acted as a lightning attraction, despite lightning rods attached to the building. Viewing an electrical storm from a mountain peak was unforgettable. Hap Conner functioned as a part-time lookout at Sinhalekin. Whenever a storm seemed imminent, he jumped on a fast horse and set out for Aeneas Mountain Lookout, a hazardous ride, because a sweaty horse attracts lightning. Once at the lookout, Hap sat on an insulated stool and watched for strikes. Because that station had no telephone, he recorded the location of strikes and reported them later from his home station, or to another guard station by heliograph — Morse code sent by flashing mirrors. The lightning bolts made jagged blazes in the sky and sometimes struck and jolted the stove inside the station. St. Elmo's Fire danced along the rails of the catwalk outside, and big balls of flame rolled eerily down the guy wires that secured the building. (St. Elmo's Fire is not flame, but a charge of electricity that appears as a round flash of light. Not only is it seen along wires and rails, but around horses' manes and people's heads.)

Skip Conner, Hap's son and a Forest Service employee, said that the smell of burnt ozone was heavy during a storm. He described a trip through a mountain pass, where low-hanging clouds scudded swiftly along and the static electricity was so intense that the hair on his arms stood up and the hair on his head prickled in response. Every time the lightning flashed, little trees would respond with an airy "whoosh" from the concussion of the following thunder. "Each time it struck near us, it added ten miles to my speed in getting out of there," grinned Conner.

For forty years or more, until the advent of helicopters and fixed-wing aircraft, the Forest Rangers lived such lonely, rigorous, and often hazardous lives, their chief companions being saddle horses and pack mules. There were no roads — even wagon roads — until homesteaders pushed up the main valleys on both sides of the North Cascades. As logging of the Forest Service lands increased, private companies did build crude roads to gain access to timber; in fact, government contracts frequently required logging firms to build roads to their specifications and leave them in good order for Forest Service use, when the logging was completed.

In 1932, with the growth of recreational use of the mountains, Clinton C. Clarke of California suggested in an article in *The Pacific Crest Trailway* that a trail be built from the Mexican to Canadian borders along the summit of the Sierras and Cascades for the use of hikers. During Depression days, between 1933 and 1942, the federal Civilian Conservation Corps hired unemployed young men for public works, planting trees, building dams, constructing trails, and similar projects. Because Clarke's proposal fit neatly into the format of CCC, it was approved as a project. By 1937, much of the Cascade Crest Trail was completed — 483 miles of it within Washington. This north-south trail was very useful to the Rangers as a link between access routes, most of which ran east and west.

When trails or roads made it possible to get close to the high mountain country, the Ranger was able to live part of the time with his family in a cabin provided by the government at the fringes of the wilderness he patrolled. The Ranger went into the mountains on horseback for days, even weeks at a time, until mid-century when aerial surveillance became so effective that there was little need of personal inspection of the forests.

Until recreational use of the mountains increased sharply after 1950, and trails were built with the public in mind, forest trails were not for pleasure, just for access. Even though the Forest Service trails were used frequently, the budget for maintenance was minimal, often restricted to only enough to enable a man and horse to get through.

Traveling a series of interlocking segments of trail, it was possible to ride from Newhalem to the Methow Valley along a route similar to that of today's North Cascades Highway. Mount Baker Forest Service personnel used the trail to maintain contact with the Okanogan administrators, especially because there were overlapping areas high in the mountains where Mount Baker administered some of Okanogan's territory, and vice versa, because arrangement of terrain made it more practical. The cross-mountain trail often clung to the mountainsides, with a precipice inches from the feet of the saddle horses. In places the horseman crossed rushing streams on slippery, moss-covered log bridges, some of which still stand only a few yards from the modern concrete highway.

Perhaps the old Granite Creek segment was the most disagreeable part of the trail system. Adjacent to the stream, the path went through a tunnel of dark, wet, overhanging trees for nineteen long miles, often covered by two or three inches of water. Built in Depression days when labor was cheap and materials expensive, the crews had built puncheon sections across the worst bogs, logs laid side by side as a "corduroy" road. Forest Service horses were shod with corks (nail-soled shoes) to enable them to grip these makeshift bridges. By the 1950s, when horses still were the usual mode of travel, the puncheon was rotted out and there was no money for now expensive labor. Trail crews threw rocks into the worst holes. Harold Chriswell, supervisor of the Mount Baker National Forest from 1957–71, who rode those treacherous trails with inspection groups of seven or eight men, commented:

"I remember horses getting into holes so deep they practically went out of sight. They would go threshing around and pieces of old puncheon four feet long would surface. Lots of horses broke legs."

A hazard along many trails in the midsummer months was the presence of yellowjackets that built nests in the dust. When the first rider over a trail stirred up a nest, there was pandemonium for a few minutes while indignant yellowjackets attacked frantic men and horses. Soon it became the custom for the first rider, when sighting yellowjackets, to yell "Bees!" and spur his horse into a gallop — then everyone clattered along the trail full speed for a while outdistancing the bees.

The custom was hard on novice riders. In 1959, Chriswell took an inspector from the Portland Regional Office to look at the forests. The inspector was a poor horseman and drew an equally poor horse from the government pool — a big, clumsy pinto named "Meatball." It was a bad year for yellowjackets; and the unfortunate rider had difficulty holding onto the horse every time the leader of the party yelled "Bees!"

"Worse yet," Chriswell said later, "Meatball knew the word and every time he heard it, he bolted. I must confess we yelled 'bees' several times an hour, just to watch this guy, who sat on his horse like a sack of potatoes."

There were bears, too, but they seldom bothered the riders. Horses could smell them in time to alert riders long before they could be seen, and the bears generally fled from people. Cougars or mountain lions were another matter — not in the high country, where the lithe and beautiful cat hunted small game — but in the valleys, where aging cougars, too slow to catch wild creatures, turned to slower domestic animals or even man. A Skagit pioneer stated that he walked from his neighbor's home to his own one night in 1919 and had the eerie feeling that something was following him. Returning to investigate his trail in the morning, he found that, superimposed on each of his footprints, was that of a big cougar.

A year later, Grace Stafford was a cook in a logging camp near Rockport, sharing a rickety cabin with another woman. One evening an unnerving scream at the flimsy cabin window brought the two women to their feet, hearts pounding. Grace bravely slammed shut the wooden shutter that hung from the glazed window, leaving the spitting and clawing cougar clinging to the window ledge outside. The terrified women added their shrieks to that of the cougar, and after what seemed like an eternity, a logger in a nearby shack came to investigate the commotion. He yelled and frightened off the cougar. After tracking the animal for seven miles the next morning, men found that it had brought down a small calf on a homesteader's farm and was gorging itself.

Four years later, in the Methow Valley, a cougar turned mankiller terrorized an entire community for weeks. It had been an exceptionally cold winter, and in December, 1924, it was nineteen degrees below zero. The wind howled incessantly, creating an even lower chill factor — a "blue northern" to the local people. Just before Christmas, Mr. and Mrs. Robert Nash, who lived at the head of a canyon below Dent Mountain near Brewster, were returning from picking up their daughter at the train station when their old Ford stalled on the hill to their home. They walked home, laughing and talking in a holiday mood, and sent Jimmy Fahlhaber, a thirteen-year-old boy who lived with them, to fetch a neighbor, Mr. Kelly, to pull the car home with his workhorses.

"Don't go through the canyon," admonished Nash. "Jacob [son of Ulrich Fries] says that something has been carrying off his sheep lately."

But it was cold out, and Jimmy was in a hurry. Hesitating only a moment, Jimmy shrugged and headed for the canyon path. The woods were already darkening in the watery light of a winter afternoon.

When Jimmy didn't return within a reasonable time, Nash became nervous and went to look for the boy. By then it was quite dark. Going to the phone, Nash rang the emergency alarm for the country line — five short rings. Everyone hearing it was supposed to answer. Neighbor Jacob Fries saddled up his best horse and galloped off to round up a search party. While other neighbors gathered, Mr. Kelly, rifle in hand, vainly searched the canyon and an old abandoned cabin, then went on to Nash's. Nash took a big gas lantern and Jimmy's dog and, with the search party, returned to the canyon, because Jimmy definitely was not along the road. At the place where Jimmy had been attacked, the dog suddenly sat down and howled eerily, then led the horrified party to Jimmy's remains. From the tracks in the snow searchers were able to reconstruct what had happened. Only a hundred yards into the wooded canyon a cougar had rushed up and jumped on Jimmy's back. Wounded, Jimmy apparently staggered to his feet and managed to draw his hunting knife. He ran a few steps before the beast hit him again and killed him, then dragged him beneath an overhanging cliff where he devoured parts of the body.

Searchers immediately put together a fund and hired a professional tracker, Boyd Hildebrand, who noticed that the cougar had a missing toe. After combing the ragged hills for such a beast for several weeks, Hildebrand came upon an old female cougar with a missing toe and shot her. Meanwhile, Wash Vanderpool of Winthrop had found a snarling cougar caught by one foot in his trap line. In the process of skinning the cat, Vanderpool found hair balls with long, blonde hairs like Jimmy's in the cougar's stomach, and concluded that *he* had found the true culprit. The skin was displayed for some time at Brewster as being from "the cougar that killed the Fahlhaber boy." Because the animal's foot had been mangled by the trap, there was no way of telling if it had a toe missing or not. Controversy continues to this day as to which one was the killer cougar. At any rate, this incident is one of the very few authenticated cases of an attack on a human being by a cougar.

Riders in the Okanogan Forest on the east side of the North Cascades had little trouble finding feed for their horses along the trails that led through open forest, but on the west side the dense timber yielded sparse forage and the Forest Service bought hay for trail use. The main pool of horses and mules was held near Ruby Creek and the Skagit River, where bottomlands provided some pasture. When Seattle City Light built Ross Dam, a clause in the Federal Power Commission permit required City Light to furnish ten tons of hay annually to the Forest Service, because of flooding the grazing grounds. This odd provision lasted almost twenty years until 1957. Seattle City Light amiably cooperated with the Forest Service, too, in transferring horses, hay, and supplies to points along Ross Lake by bringing them over the dam and onto boats.

Besides the hazards of bad trails, bees, and cougars, trail

riders often encountered snow in the mountains. Many of the mountain passes were at 5,000 feet elevation or more and did not become clear of snow until July; in fact, snow has been recorded at that elevation on every day of some year. On a day in early summer, Harold Chriswell and six people set out to rendezvous with Okanogan Forest representatives in Hart's Pass to inspect grazing ranges. The trail from Ross skirted along the high mountains near Canyon Creek, then climbed over Jackita Mountain. Below the summit a huge snow slide covered the trail for half a mile on a downhill slope. First a brittle cornice had to be knocked down and, as the snow was fairly soft and provided footing, Chriswell recalled, "When it came to deciding who was to go first, no one volunteered. Nobody said he wouldn't go; he just didn't start. As it was my group, I had to go first." Fortunately his horse was calm and, in a series of half leaps, he made it to solid trail. The packer, Phil Taylor, laid the reins over the necks of his mules and talked them down, calling each one by name.

The party was a day late for the rendezvous, but the Okanogan group was waiting in Devil's Pass, one day's ride west of Hart's Pass.

As the North Cascades became visited by more hikers and mountain climbers, the Rangers and other forest personnel had to search for lost people. One of the most chilling and mysterious searches resulted from the discovery in July, 1951, of a note tacked up on a tree in Cascade Pass:

> Help. We are lost in a blizzard and out of food and
> only God can help us. The Perkinses.

The note was dated March, 1951, a time when the pass had been choked with snow. Furthermore, no one had reported any Perkinses missing and the search revealed no skeletons of the people. The mystery remains.

Even close to civilization the mountains sometimes claimed victims. In September, 1941, two couples, carrying sleeping bags, started out on a hike from Newhalem to the top of Sourdough Mountain above Diablo Lake. Soon tiring, Mr. and Mrs. Conrad Opitz stopped to rest, while Mr. and Mrs. Clarence Hale went on to the top of the mountain to an old lookout tower. Leaving his wife to make a fire, Mr. Hale returned to search for the other couple. He found that Mr. Opitz had become so exhausted he could not walk. In the growing darkness, Hale and Mrs. Opitz tried to help her husband down the trail but Mr. Opitz collapsed. When it began to snow, Hale went on down the trail alone to seek help, while Opitz and his wife settled down in their sleeping bags.

About dawn Conrad Opitz began muttering deliriously, and Mrs. Opitz was so chilled that she could not undo the fastenings on her sleeping bag and make a fire. When the morning sun warmed her a bit, she was able to free herself and staggered up to the lookout tower where Mrs. Hale remained. Leaving Mrs. Opitz in the warm tower, Mrs. Hale went down the trail but was unable to locate either man, so continued to Diablo, where she collapsed after telling her story. A rescue party found both men dead of hypothermia. Hale had wandered off the trail and was wrapped only in a single blanket; Opitz had died in his sleeping bag. The women survived the ordeal partly because they were clad in wool clothing, while the men were lightly dressed.

When helicopter pilots took over much of the forest patrol by 1965, many trails were allowed to return to foliage. Although helicopters may fly over the wilderness for patrol, they may not land unless lives are endangered or fire protection requires it. The use of power saws, bulldozers, and motorized ground transportation is forbidden, too, unless a dangerous fire makes it mandatory. Even then, a Forest Service District must obtain permission from Washington, D.C., for each deviation. Therefore, maintenance of trails has regressed to the midcentury method of using horses, mules and hand tools. Because the working season in the high country is so short, critics sometimes chafe at the regulations, pointing out that it takes four days travel to do one day's repair in some cases.

Today's trails fit in with the land contours, incorporating steep slopes at times to avoid cutting trees or chopping up land — a gradual change within the last ten years from the old specifications, which called for grades of not more than three per cent on a Forest Service trail. A unique type of trail crew has appeared — backpackers armed only with light shovels and tools, who roam the trails for weeks without returning to base. Four wilderness rangers operate out of Winthrop on foot, staying out for ten days at a time. Their job is to inform hikers and horsemen and to see that regulations are complied with.

The mountains are being cleared of the debris of decades — old mining machinery, ancient camp materials, parts of crashed aircraft. Only a few years ago, all debris was buried, but the bears dug everything up to examine it for edibility. Bears also ate the stained cedar signs along the trails; currently signs are made from one-and-one-quarter-inch rough oak, with the message routed or burned into the wood. Bears don't like oak. One time a bear bit into a spray can of blue paint in a Forest Service cabin in the Pasayten Wilderness and left the whole interior splattered with blue dots. A camper at Bridge Creek Camp above Stehekin accidentally discovered a cure for camp-marauding bears. He left camp one morning leaving only canned goods within reach. Upon his return he found their punctured remains — including a pressurized spray can of insect repellant — and the tracks, right over the top of his flattened tent, of a hastily retreating bear who had bitten into the can.

Evolving from the access trails of the Forest Service, an extensive trail system has been developed as increasing areas of the North Cascades are traveled by the public. Such trails range from those used by casual one-day hikers to steep, high-altitude routes among the crags, many of which are connected by the Pacific Crest Trail. Since the completion of the North Cascades Highway, hikers can intercept the latter where it crosses near Rainy Pass.

13

Firefighters and the Smokejumper Brigade

Fire control was one of the most formidable tasks of the Forest Service. For centuries, fires set by lightning had raged unchecked over the North Cascades every summer, darkening Northwest skies with a pall of smoke. Early explorers mentioned the difficulty of seeing the mountains; and old-timers recall that in the summers of their childhood the skies were always obscured. In 1868, travelers on the Skagit River said the visibility was so poor one could not see a boat's length ahead; and that they had seen birds drop out of the sky suffocated by smoke.

There was no simple solution. In the early years of its jurisdiction the Forest Service sent its men out with axes and shovels to find blazes before they got too large. With the primitive condition of trails, access was the greatest problem. For long stretches on the Skagit River, there was no way across except by "go-devil," a cable strung across the river with a cage suspended in such a way that a man could pull himself along.

In the summer of 1910, Ranger C. C. McGuire, based at Diablo Lake, could see a fire only about three miles away, but across the river from him. It took him an entire day to reach it, three days to put it out (for it had spread by then), and another day to return to base. The need for a crossing of the Skagit Gorge was critical. McGuire found a spot where the river was only thirteen feet wide at water level, "standing on edge" because above and below the Gorge the river was much wider. In this spot the canyon walls were 100 feet apart and 150 feet above the water. Miners at one time had a cable bridge across the chasm, and some of the materials were still usable. The Forest Service did not provide engineering assistance, but left to his own ingenuity, McGuire and three men built a bridge strong enough to support a pack train, which stood until Seattle City Light dynamited it during dam construction in 1924.

The Forest Service gave little respite for error and small credit for effort: when one of McGuire's superiors made an annual check of government property later, he found that the Ranger was missing a single die for his tools, and sent him a bill for one dollar.

Because the western slope of the North Cascades was wetter, fires there seldom spread rapidly; still, stubborn fires along steep ridges sometimes called for unusual methods. Volunteers from outdoor clubs or mountaineers have had to scale cliffs and lay hoses to the site of a fire from the canyon streams. One of the largest west-side fires was the Big Beaver Burn, an all-summer fire that consumed more than 40,000 acres near Ross Lake in 1926. Hubert Wilson, who was then a Forest Guard and later assistant supervisor of the Mount Baker National Forest, said the smoke hung over the area so thickly that the sun always looked blood-red. All the firefighters could do was slog in on foot or horseback and burn off fire breaks or mix the fire with dirt around the edges. The fire was too large to contain, only the fall rains could put it out.

There was a bonus, though, from the destruction — a new stand of excellent Douglas fir. Wilson, who held a master's degree in forestry, pointed out that Douglas fir seedlings must have a cleared area in which to grow — whether caused by fire or man — because they need sunlight and warmth for the seeds to germinate. Indeed, the seedlings will *never* grow under the parent trees in deep shade.

Because of sparse rainfall, blazes in the Okanogan pine forests were not the smoldering types of the Mount Baker

Forest, but often were holocausts that burned so fast a person had to run for his life before them. In August, 1929, a large fire started at Lake Chelan. Fanned by strong winds, it burned fiercely over the hills and into Methow Valley, consuming 13,000 acres. Two men were caught in the path of the blaze and never seen again. Alta Lake and the surrounding park were threatened. Firefighters were powerless to control the fire; it died out of its own accord when it came to an area of barren rock.

Smoke chasers, protective assistants, and trail crews were stationed all through the Okanogan, on call day and night. Usually the lightning storms were followed by heavy rains, so there was a two-or-three-day grace period in which to find and extinguish small blazes. Often the smoke chaser located the fire by smell, but used compass and cross-bearings provided by the lookouts; later small aircraft were used as spotters. If the chaser found the fire to be small, he could mix it with dirt or chop down the tree involved. It was the "sleepers" that caused the big fires — those that smoldered undetected for days until the forests dried out, then leaped into full–fledged blazes.

In 1939 at Winthrop, a new elite corps of firefighters was born — the smokejumpers. Prior to this time the Russians had experimented with mass parachute jumping. David Godwin, chief of fire control in Washington, D.C., obtained the literature published by them and had it translated. He persuaded the Eagle Parachute Company of Pennsylvania to furnish chutes and experienced jumpers for an experiment to see if the technique was practical for firefighting. Offered first to Region 1 in Missoula, Montana, the project was declined; but Region 6, with headquarters in Portland and covering the North Cascades, accepted the challenge, selecting the Okanogan forest as the best area to test the technique because it had bad fire scars and was rugged terrain.

In September, contractors from Eagle Parachute and hired parachutists moved into an old warehouse at the Winthrop Ranger Station, and a smoke chaser, Francis Lufkin, was assigned to the project as support man. The professional jumpers had a contract to make sixty jumps into all types of timber and terrain to gain experience in landing in forested areas. Because the parachutists frequently came down in trees and became entangled, Lufkin's job was to get them down, to return them to base in Winthrop, and to supply them with necessities. After fifty-four jumps the crew concluded that it had completed its gathering of data; and on' a "bilious, foggy, rainy day," the crew chief decided that Lufkin should make a practice jump just for the experience of doing it. Lufkin said later, "I just assumed I had to do it. I thought I might be assigned to the corps to learn smokejumping. Those fellows made $2,300 a year while I made $1,680. I had twin sons, had started to build a new house, and that extra money looked good."

While the professionals put on Lufkin's suit and parachute for him, they gave him the only instructions he had before making the jump onto the Intercity Airport. Lufkin conceded he was nervous, but only about the airplane ride, his first. He had watched all of the jumps and concluded that the parachuting would be no trouble. He added: "They told me about pulling the ripcord after a count of three, to get my body in a good position, not to wait too long, and that's about it."

During the time it took the Stinson Gullwing airplane to climb to an altitude of 3,500 feet, Lufkin kept reviewing the methods for getting his body into a good position. The chutes had long, hard, linen risers; and a man had to be sure that his head didn't get slammed by one. He had seen jumpers with vicious cuts on the sides of their heads, broken noses, and eyelids laid open. These were his only concerns as he jumped into the half-overcast sky over the Methow Valley. Everything went smoothly, and even though he was in the clouds part of the time during his descent, he maneuvered the chute onto the airport at Winthrop.

After his successful jump, Lufkin became an official smokejumper candidate. Four men began training as the Forest Service's first crew in June, 1940: two professionals, Chet Berry and Glen Smith, and two trainees, George Honey and Francis Lufkin. The four made their jumps each day at about four A.M., early enough to assure that they had time to get out of trees and back home. With luck, they were back by breakfast. Then Smith repacked the chutes while the others experimented with methods of getting themselves down from trees — the perpetual problem. Honey and Lufkin taught the two professional jumpers how to fight fires from their experiences as Forest Guards. The crew wound up the 1940 season by putting on a demonstration jump for Chief Godwin, who came from Washington, D.C., to the remote firefighter training camp at Salmon Meadows for the occasion. Godwin was delighted. Even though the test jumps were not made under actual fire conditions, the technique seemed entirely practical.

In 1941, headquarters were established for the jumpers at Intercity Airport (then just a dirt airstrip near Twisp) in a twelve-by-fourteen-foot tent. In August, Glen Smith and Lufkin made the first real firefighting jump to a blaze near Bridge Creek and the Twisp River. The method was sound, according to Lufkin:

> I used to walk for hours or days to get into a fire. It took less than 15 minutes in the airplane to get to this one, and we had it out before the trail crew reached us to take us out — a total of 7 or 8 hours in and out. A year or two earlier a similar lightning strike expanded into a 100-acre fire that cost $44,000 in materials and man-hours to put out.

In 1941, World War II erupted and expenditures for nonmilitary needs were curtailed. Instead of staffing the Winthrop smokejumper base and providing further parachute handling equipment, the Forest Service temporarily disbanded it and sent the crew, with Lufkin as squad leader, to Missoula's smokejumper base (Region 1 had relented and formed a jumper crew). There the smokejumpers already had a major parachute loft with sewing machines for repair, as well as a few aircraft for fire control use. The crews were dispatched to fires anywhere in the combined territory, including Idaho, Montana and Washington. In 1945, Norman Penick, forest supervisor for the Okanogan, concluded that such farflung travel was costly and ineffective, and that the Intercity base should be reestablished permanently. Lufkin was put in charge, remaining until his retirement. Flimsy old Civilian Conservation Corps buildings formed the first headquarters, consisting of a parachute loft, small administration building, and bunkhouses. Three years later the flood of the Methow undermined these structures, carrying off the loft and part of the gear. Only by chopping the bunkhouses in two and dragging them away from the river did the crew save its buildings. Thirty feet of the airport was lost to the rampaging river.

In the 1950s and 1960s the use of aircraft of all kinds for surveillance and fire control mushroomed. High-altitude mapping was done from fixed-wing aircraft like Beechcraft 99As or some Cessnas, until satellite programs took over in the 1970s (ERTS, Earth Resources Technology Satellite). In the 1950s old Ford Tri-Motor planes, DC-3s, and C-46s hauled jumpers, but currently, sophisticated turboprop aircraft like Neptune P2V or DC-6s are used for dropping jumpers or spreading fire retardant, commonly called borate bombing, a liquid concentrate fertilizer. The first helicopter appeared in the Okanogan Forest in 1956 on contract for smokejumper retrieval, and within two years copters were used more than sixty per cent of the time as shuttles to transport jumpers to a point where trucks could return them to base.

The latest experiment using helicopters is the "smoke slider," where a helicopter hovers over a fire and the firefighter slides down a rope onto the site. As helicopters grew more powerful, trail crews used them as aerial workhorses to lift heavy equipment, bridge girders, and other equipment. Two paramedics from Intercity now perform rescue medical work under an agreement with the Okanogan County sheriff. So efficient has this service become that a hiker or climber could be in the Twisp clinic less than two hours after injury.

Jumping into strange areas holds unexpected thrills. About midnight after putting out a fire one day in 1962, two smokejumpers from Winthrop, Tommy Thomas and Orville Varner, were hiking out to a road for pick-up when their flashlight beams picked out several sets of shiny "eyes" — some kind of animals that snorted and looked like bears. The two jumpers clambered up trees, mentally measuring grizzly bears with heads two feet wide. After spending an uncomfortable, frightening night in the trees, the two men climbed stiffly down at dawn, only to find that they were in a pasture surrounded by curious Black Angus cattle. The shiny ear clips on the cows had reflected the light and appeared like wide-set eyes.

It was not unusual to encounter bears, but the bears usually ran away. One pair of jumpers came down in the middle of an elk herd, and a third almost on top of a hunter who was stalking the elk, nearly startling the man into a heart attack. In 1956, there were fires everywhere, set by a rash of lightning storms. Harassed dispatchers gave orders to the jumpers, "Jump on anything that's burning. Don't wait for specific directions." To their intense embarrassment, two jumpers landed in the middle of a Girl Scout camp, where the youngsters were singing around a campfire.

During World War II most of the smokejumper trainees were conscientious objectors, but in 1946 the Forest Service began to receive veteran paratroopers. They required just as much training as novices, however, because the equipment and methods of operation were different. Frank Berry, a Forest Service employee, was the first to develop chutes using open gores for stability.

One of the worst fire episodes in Okanogan history occurred during the last two weeks of July, 1970, when 198 recorded lightning strikes set fires. More than 5,000 people were involved in the firefighting operation during the peak of the period, including 200 smokejumpers. The nation's elite came from everywhere: the Bitterroot Hotshots from Montana, Scottie's Raiders from the Pike National Forest in Colorado, the Colville and Spokane Indian Firefighters, Cree and Sioux from Montana, Apaches from New Mexico, Hopi and Navajo from Arizona, and Mexican-American crews from New Mexico, California, and Oregon. So many aircraft were working out of little Intercity Airport that the Federal Aviation Administration sent in a traffic controller to operate a "tower" from the back of a truck, twenty-four hours a day. Crews arriving were also landed at Omak Airport, where the Air National Guard furnished a mobile air traffic control unit.

Several mobile fire weather stations manned by Weather Bureau personnel were installed in the mountains to provide up-to-the-minute information for planes. It was one of the largest air operations in Forest Service history. During one day, twenty-three helicopters and twenty-four fixed-wing airplanes were in use. Eighteen aerial tankers dropped over a half million gallons of retardant. An F4H jet fighter bomber from distant Mountain Home Air Force Base in California came to deliver infra-red imagery to firefighting strategists, a method that shows the varying intensities of temperature as different colors on a scanner. In this way, analysts can determine the location of fires or where forests are becoming so dry and hot that combustion is imminent. From the Army at Fort Lewis, Washington, came one-hundred fifty-five men and sixty-five vehicles to provide a field kitchen, laundry, showers, transportation, and general support for the men in the forests. The worst single fire covered 6,000 acres east of Winthrop, and as many as sixty or seventy men were dropped on blazes at one time. Francis Lufkin's own daughter was caught in one fire area, a lookout station on Buck Peak. At immense expense the fires were extinguished.

Although the maintenance of well-trained smokejumper crews, late-model aircraft, and sophisticated surveillance techniques is costly, the value of timber saved in the national forests and the preservation of irreplaceable scenic assets greatly offsets the expenditures. On the ground, the completion of the North Cascades Highway in 1972 provided at least one high-speed access route to the heart of the mountains for firefighting — the first artery that has permitted the transfer of motorized equipment rapidly from one side of the range to the other. Because most serious fires are set by lightning, even the watchfulness of Forest Rangers over campers and motorists will not eliminate the likelihood of sudden blazes in the National Park and the other forest areas.

XXXXXXXXXXXXXXXXXXXXXXXXXX

14

Electrical Power and Politics

The Skagit River, coursing free and wild through the precipitous Gorge, was both friend and enemy to the North Cascadians — a friend because it provided an avenue into the wilderness, an enemy because it often flooded their homesteads.

As early as 1905 a power prospector, Charles Freeman of Anacortes, stopped at the Davis Inn on Cedar Bar (Diablo Lake) and examined the crude generating plant of the Davis family. He looked at the volume of water surging through the Gorge, which was as narrow as thirteen feet in places, and went home to organize financial backing for a dam. With three Denver capitalists, E. M. Biggs, M. W. Patrick, and J. S. McCrystal, Freeman formed the Skagit Power Company.

Federal regulations governing power sites were complex. Before any work could commence, a firm had to post a claim on a proposed site, then file an application for a permit, which described the work contemplated; but, if no work was done, others could and did file on the same claim as soon as the permit expired — while the original claimant also asked for renewal. In the Skagit Canyon, the center of power interest, the result was a monumental snarl of superimposed claims which the county had to sort out, delaying real work for months. Often companies or individuals filed on numerous sites, just to shut out potential competitors for a while. The newly organized Skagit Power Company filed on several locations, including Box Canyon — which they renamed Diablo Canyon after its namesake in Arizona. Under the direction of C. L. Milton, a civil engineer from Colorado, Skagit Power started work on a large dam and built camps for their laborers. To supply them, the firm also tried to build a road from the site to the Skagit Valley, but was defeated — as every builder had been — by the walls of the Gorge.

Because lack of access made construction so slow, Freeman ordered all work on the dam stopped in the middle of 1909 and filed on additional power sites from Newhalem to Ruby Creek. These were no more accessible than Diablo; so in 1910, Skagit Power entirely ceased operations on the Skagit River and, two years later, sold its claims to Puget Sound Traction, Power & Light Company, a subsidiary of a large Boston holding company, Stone & Webster.

This big firm immediately filed for a two-year permit with the Department of Agriculture; but, even though the permit cost them more than $5,000, Stone & Webster did no work whatever within the period, turning their attention to the Baker River near Concrete. During this time the firm was charged with monopoly because it had been buying up power sites all over the State. It defeated the accusation and, when its permit expired and no one else had applied, the company was allowed to renew it for three more years. At this point Seattle City Light came out of the wings to protest. Because its hydroelectric project on the Cedar River south of Seattle was too small, Seattle had been exploring the possibility of harnessing the Skagit River. The original protest was ignored but, when the permit again expired in 1917, James Delmage Ross of Seattle City Light jumped in to file a permit on August 7, 1917, on the basis that Stone & Webster had done no work at all on the sites, that it merely had tied them up.

The plot thickened. Stone & Webster, reacting to Ross's claims, proceeded to buy the land around sites on which City Light had made claims. In September, Ross traveled to Washington, D.C., to place his application for a permit before David F. Houston, Secretary of Agriculture, and to object to the tactics of Stone & Webster as merely obstructionist. City Light's permit called for a system that would produce

25,000 kilowatts; Houston decided in its favor, asking for proof of financial ability of Seattle to complete the project and a set of plans before he gave his final approval.

In January, 1918, the City Council of Seattle appropriated five million dollars for the construction of a power plant on the Skagit, and the government gave them until May to decide on a definite site. Until then, the river was theirs to explore. Four months was not much time to survey a complicated waterway and make plans affecting Seattle's electrical supply for years to come. Ross — half practical, half politician — proposed that a smaller dam be built first at Gorge Creek to provide some power, both for Seattle and for the construction site of a larger dam at Ruby Creek. On February 13, 1918, little more than a month after receiving his tentative permit, Ross made his final application for those two dams at an estimated cost of $16,768,165. Years later, he admitted that he didn't really believe that a dam should be built at Ruby then, because it would develop too much of the Skagit River's potential power at one time; but he needed to file some specific plans in order to secure the final permit.

Seattle's citizens received the news of this potential cost with dismay. Sidewalk critics cried that the Skagit River was too big and too far distant and that, in any case, the cost could not be approved without the Capital Issues Committee's sanction, which would take too long. Dredged up for sensational charges was the fact that some of those urging a Skagit dam had built the original Cedar Falls Dam for Seattle, a project that had been a disaster because it — well, it simply leaked. Geologists had not done their homework, and the lake behind the dam continued to dribble out slowly. Would this happen at the Skagit, too, dribbling out the taxpayers' money?

After further, more complete surveying of the Skagit, Seattle City Light was granted a conditional permit in May after the city had appropriated an additional half-million dollars.

City engineer Arthur Dimock established an outpost at Gorge Creek. Because an access road still was deemed impractical, he moved in his construction equipment from road's end at Damnation Creek by scow one and one-half miles to Thornton Creek, then dragged the material over a skid road to the dam site. The scow's gas engine was unable to manage the heavier loads, so the operator had to fasten the scow to ropes tied to trees upstream and, using a big spool on deck, winch himself up the river. Workers were housed temporarily in the abandoned buildings of the Skagit Queen Mining Company on Thunder Creek, and some lived in tents. In 1919, Seattle City Light bought the municipal holdings of Puget Sound Traction, Power & Light Company in Seattle.

Consulting geologist Henry Landes had warned that during the Ice Age there had been a natural lake at the site of Ross Lake, that it was probable deep deposits of gravel existed in the bed of the Skagit. Drilling confirmed his theories; the gravel was more than one hundred feet thick! Somewhat downstream from the selected site, gravel was only sixty-three feet thick, but there the dam would be so much higher that it would cost thirty million dollars. Ross knew that the citizens of Seattle would never buy this concept and explored again near the mouth of Ruby Creek. The delays in site selection caused mutters of discontent in Seattle.

As World War I ended, the matter still had not been resolved nor the final permit issued. Labor costs rose sharply and Ross revised his estimated cost for the project from five million dollars to almost ten million. When drillers finally found a site with good bedrock for footings, Ross went before the City Council and convinced them the dam would be worthwhile, even at the greater cost. The Council voted to proceed, appropriating $432,900 to build a wagon road from Rockport to the dam site, a small sawmill, and a temporary power plant. Carl F. Uhden was appointed to supervise the project.

Elated Skagit Valley citizens viewed this decision as a step toward their long-awaited road to the Methow Valley, but it was not to be. Uhden concluded that a road would be far too expensive and that a railroad from Rockport would be better. Ross concurred. Some believed that his reason was that the builders could control ingress to the project, restricting the intrusion of outsiders. A contract was given to Mandic Construction Company to build roadbed between Rockport, where the Great Northern ended, and the Gorge; but that firm went bankrupt and the contract went to Grant Smith Construction of Portland. A final permit was issued to Seattle City Light on May 27, 1920, to build the twenty-five-foot concrete dam at Gorge Creek, with a reservoir, a two-mile tunnel, and a temporary crib dam on Newhalem Creek to provide power for the site. The Ruby Dam was postponed.

The work force became almost 500 men, as the project developed. Many families joined the men to live near Newhalem. There were children to be educated and a public school opened with joint financing by the county and City Light. Other amenities followed. In April, 1921, the Bellingham Presbytery assigned to the camp a roving minister who had worked in the logging camps, Reverend L. H. Peterson, Parson Pete. He organized not only church services but well-attended social events and published a newsy little paper called *Fits and Starts*. As the settlement grew to about 1,000 people, some still living in tents, there were endless debates about the name of the town — Goodell's or Newhalem. College students hired to work for the summer settled the issue forever. Just prior to the arrival of a group of Seattle officials, the students hung a big plank sign at the entrance to camp, saying "Welcome to Newhalem." After that, it was Newhalem, a name that is not derived from New Halem but Ne-whalem, an Indian name meaning goat trap.

The railroad reached the town in April, 1921, and moved toward Gorge Creek, two and one-half miles away. When the crews reached the infamous Devil's Corner, site of the Goat Trail, the contractor built a bridge to the south side to avoid struggling with the precipice. Because the approach was crooked, the historic corner was dubbed the Devil's Elbow. When construction began on the dam, Seattle City Light built an incline railway to provide access to the lake above. For years thereafter until the present time, this sturdy workhorse, traveling 600 feet of cog track, towed incredible loads of material up the side of the mountain — a sixty-eight per cent grade and a vertical lift of 313 feet. Tourists, workmen, inspectors — all went up the cog.

The railroad from Rockport to Gorge Creek was in operation by the fall of 1921, with City Light using a World War I surplus gasoline motor car purchased from Fort Lewis. The twenty-five passenger train soon became known in the Skagit as the "Toonerville Trolley." For freight the company used a gasoline powered freight car, a three-truck rail flatcar and a ten-ton flatcar trailer. In 1922 the railway was modified between Newhalem and Gorge Creek to use electricity, furnished by three electric engines and a rotary unit at the Newhalem powerhouse.

When the R. C. Storrie Company of San Francisco was awarded a contract to build the Gorge power tunnel, it brought narrow-gauge equipment for the job. In order to use the existing tracks, a third rail between the standard rails was added.

The railroad was subject to the vagaries of weather, never gentle in the North Cascades. Floods often washed out roadbed or deep mud and snow covered the tracks. Heavy rains in 1922 washed out some of the rails, and when crews repairing the damage found traces of gold in the rocks on the right-of-way, they deserted their jobs to prospect.

Storrie's contract to build the tunnel was disastrous financially for the firm. The company installed big air compressors and eight-inch pipe at Newhalem to carry compressed air two miles to the jackhammers drilling at Gorge Creek. However, Seattle City Light had a strange "squeeze" on Storrie. The city had first claim to the power output of the small temporary power plant; yet a clause in its contract with Storrie exacted penalties of $500 per day for delays in completion of the tunnel. Storrie had to vie with City Light, at times, for power to run its equipment, thus experiencing delays through no fault of its own. When the company finished the job, it submitted a bill for $290,000 more than the original bid because of delays, but only received $88,000 from City Light — and then only after filing suit. In 1924 workers picked up the third rail from the railroad and left the Skagit, no doubt with considerable relief.

Because the dam was supposed to be in use by September, 1923, for a cost of five million dollars — then seven or eight million (and finally by 1924 eleven million) — the citizens of Seattle grew restless. Especially under attack in the newspapers was the cost of two million for installing the railroad, which the *Seattle Star* insisted was not authorized by the city. The paper demanded an official investigation, and Mayor Edwin J. Brown agreed to appoint Phillip Tindall, chairman of the Utilities Committee of the City Council. Disappointing the critics, Tindall found that the railroad was the best way to get into the site, rather than a wagon road, and cleared everyone involved of graft. He blamed the increased cost on the rising expense of labor and materials after the war; the delays caused by inexperience, weather, terrain, and a certain amount of "muddle."

While the political and journalistic smoke swirled, engineers still struggled to get electricity flowing. In December, 1923, the powerhouse was finished. Two generators were being installed by Westinghouse of Pittsburgh, and the two turbines were expected to be delivered from S. Morgan Smith of New York. At that late date Supervisor Uhden decided to build the Gorge diversion dam and intake from heavy timbers rather than the masonry originally planned, in order to save money. Uhden received a final $177,000 to finish the dam and intake.

In the meantime, during 1922 and 1923, one hundred miles of transmission line had been built across country from the Skagit Gorge to Seattle — no mean feat in itself. To facilitate communication, Seattle City Light also added direct telephone lines. Something was hooked up wrong; and when the switch was thrown on the two generators at the Gorge powerhouse for testing, every telephone on every Forest Service District of the North Cascades rang, bringing all the Rangers onto the line. The problem was easily remedied; the Forest Service phones simply had a common ground with the generators.

Despite all the boondoggles and delays, on September 14, 1924, Seattle received its first 5,000 kilowatts from the Gorge powerhouse. National attention focused on the project when President Calvin Coolidge pressed a gold key at the White House which sent a signal over the Postal Telegraph Cable Company's wires to the offices of Seattle City Light, and from there over the phone system to the Skagit to start the turbines and generators humming. Formal operation of the plant began at six-fifteen P.M. Pacific Standard Time. Simultaneously with the beginning, a signal caused a whistle to blow in Seattle at the Lake Union steam plant.

Controversies during the project between Supervisor Carl Uhden and the City of Seattle resulted in Uhden's resignation on December 31, 1924, after the completion of the job; but the city, typically, had the last word and cut off his pay as of December 1.

Despite the high cost of the dam, the two generators on the Skagit supplied Seattle with more electricity during 1925 than had all other sources in 1924.

Because a water storage dam was needed to hold back some of the Skagit's water for use during low water periods, Diablo Dam was designed and construction started immediately after Gorge. Also, Bonneville Dam was not yet completed, so Seattle's increasing need for electrical power gave Diablo priority. The city operated in a bootstrap financial climate, where increasing revenues from sale of electric power had to provide the funds for expansion.

In 1925 Seattle created a three-man power commission to supervise the pursuit of Ross's three-dam plan — Diablo, Ross, and High Gorge (a new one, not the diversion dam) in that order. As soon as the Federal Power Commission license was obtained, Ross negotiated with the Canadian government for use of the land just north of the international border beyond Ross Lake, which would be flooded eventually. Two private 340-acre parcels in Canada were purchased, as well, and held until such time as they were needed.

Narrow Diablo Canyon was a natural location for a dam; the site selected was only nineteen feet wide at river level. With the advice and consulting services of a private civil engineering firm, Constant Angle Arch Dam Company, the City of Seattle's engineering office designed Diablo, the largest constant arch dam anywhere in the world at the time — 389 feet high, 147 feet thick at the base, and 1180 feet long on the crest.

Meantime, more political maneuvering kept Seattleites stirred up. Stone & Webster had been supplying Tacoma for years with sufficient power when, for some unannounced reason, the firm suddenly cut them off, claiming a shortage of power for Seattle. J. D. Ross lost no time in offering to provide a tie-in between Seattle and Tacoma for interchange of power, implementing the system in 1923. Too late, Stone & Webster (through its subsidiary, Puget Sound Power & Light) realized its tactical error and attacked City Light's action in the courts. It threw thousands of dollars — reportedly $126,000 in 1924 alone — into an effort to prevent Seattle City Light's actions. U.S. Senator Homer T. Bone introduced a bill to legalize the intercity connection and to authorize the sale of power outside of Seattle's corporate limits, but his bill was defeated.

Puget Sound Power contributed $60,000 a year for three consecutive years to Voters Information League, which attacked municipal power in various ways, even making an anti-public-power movie. Ross and City Light's reply to the propaganda was the reduction of power rates as soon as additional dams were complete. The more Ross reduced rates, the more power he sold, acquiring four times as many customers as his private power rival. Replying to the lost taxes argument, City Light pointed out that consumers were saving ten million dollars a year in power costs, more than all municipal taxes, and demanded that Puget Sound Power sell out to Seattle City Light. Stone & Webster, the parent company — an enormous national concern — became more than a little irked at upstart Seattle.

Because Ross was in the limelight so often, he was becoming better known than most of Seattle's mayors and some of them resented him. A candidate for mayor, Frank Edwards, visited with Stone & Webster on the East Coast in February, 1930, just before his election in March and received the red carpet treatment. Nothing about the visit became public; but one year after his election, Edwards summarily dismissed Ross on vague charges of extravagance, professional incompetence, and of building his own political empire. Ross did not deign to reply but quietly went on vacation, leaving behind a civic uproar. A widespread movement to recall Mayor Edwards developed, led by young attorney Marion A. Zioncheck. Citizens circulated petitions, bought advertising space, and gained the support of the powerful Hearst newspapers in their campaign to unseat the mayor. Edwards was removed from office on July 13, 1931, with a recall vote of 125,000 to 15,000; and his successor promptly restored Ross to office. Ross returned to his Skagit Project affairs, where Diablo Dam was rising.

Because of the experience gained during construction of Gorge Dam in Skagit Canyon, the building of Diablo went smoothly except for problems in diverting the huge volume of water in the Skagit during construction. Contrary to usual dam-building procedure, contractors built inward from each side of the canyon walls, which provided excellent anchorage for the foundations. The river ran free until it was absolutely necessary to divert the flow and complete the center of the dam.

Employees working on the dam project lived either in Newhalem or in camps above Diablo Dam, one at Hollywood, a tongue-in-cheek name given to the camp because a woman named Clara Bow lived there. The men ate in a common cookhouse. There was little else to attract workers to the remote canyon, so the food was superb and plentiful. To serve the needs of visiting officials, a small hostel, inelegantly named the Hillbilly Hotel, was run by Jack Ferrar and his wife. Ferrar had worked as a watchman for the Chancellor Mine on Slate Creek during the gold rush and, when it suspended operations, he came to work for City Light. After the Diablo Dam was finished, Ferrar moved on to a job in Seattle, but Mrs. Ferrar had fallen in love with the North Cascades so deeply that she and her terrier Angus lived for six months each summer in happy solitude at the Chancellor caretaker's cabin. She painted the birds and flowers of the mountains and took nature photos. Unfortunately, her collection seems to have been lost. In October, 1947, she and Angus started out of the mountains via Hart's Pass, but they had stayed too long. A few days afterward, they were found by searchers, lying in the snow along the trail, dead of exposure. Some said that's the way the aging woman would have wanted it, to lie forever in the North Cascades.

Other than occasional problems with high water and the inevitable construction accidents, Diablo moved ahead swiftly. One of the most gruesome accidents was the collapse of scaffolding on the dam as concrete was being poured, burying three men. Following an old custom, workers buried a silver dollar in the dam for each man killed on the job. Water backed up behind the dam as it rose; and in March, 1932, heavy rains in the high mountains sent a flood down the entire Skagit River, causing City Light to post watchmen over its new dam.

Fifty-five miles downstream in the little hamlet of Lyman a rumor started — probably from a gossipmonger on the party telephone lines — that a crack had developed in Diablo and the dam might burst at any moment. The news leaped through the community and nearby Birdsview, as well. Visualizing a wall of water rolling down the valley, the Lyman Fire Department blew its fire siren and spread word of the emergency. Every resident grabbed what he could and took to the hills. Residents of Mount Vernon and Burlington viewed the rumor skeptically, but some moved to higher ground. Through it all, the upriver towns of Concrete, Van Horn, Marblemount, and others — which would indeed have been decimated if the dam had burst — blissfully went about their daily routines because telephone lines were down and no word of impending doom had reached anyone. When nothing happened and no one could verify how the rumor had started, sheepish Lyman residents returned to their homes.

With the stock market crash of 1929, funds disappeared. Ross was caught with his turbines and related equipment sitting in crates at the dam site and no money to install them. Despite the respect he enjoyed from President Roosevelt,

Ross tried in vain to get federal funds from the Reconstruction Finance Company in 1932 and 1933. Having exhausted governmental sources, Ross went to Wall Street and laid his problem before Guy C. Myers, investment banker, and got his money. A syndicate was formed; bonds were issued for almost five million dollars, and debentures were sold on May 1, 1934. Ross completed his powerhouse, as well as part of a new office building in Seattle to house the expanding City Light offices. President Roosevelt pressed a key at his Hyde Park home in November, 1936, to start power flowing to Seattle.

It was clear that Ross's heart, as well as his head, was in the Skagit Canyon. He had persuaded the designers of Diablo to lower the main floor of the powerhouse to enable visitors to see the big generators at work. An amateur naturalist, Ross imported exotic plants and flowers for Ladder Falls Garden behind the Gorge powerhouse at Newhalem. Because of his theory that plants would eventually adapt to a new environment, he installed hot-water pipes throughout the gardens to heat the soil for the semitropical plants he had purchased — pending their adjustment to a cool climate. He experimented with oranges and grapefruit and fully expected to develop a variety of pineapple that would thrive in the upper Skagit. Whenever he traveled, he picked up seeds or plants that might grow there. From Lincoln's tomb he got several small oak trees, from Mount Vernon two trees which he named George and Martha, and from Hyde Park two named Franklin and Eleanor. Ross also installed a small zoo at Diablo adjacent to Hollywood, where residents and tourists were entertained by monkeys, tame deer, peacocks, cockatoos, swans, and an infamous butting goat. But one by one, the birds vanished, victims of wild animals appreciative of gourmet specials in the wilderness.

Through his conferences with Ross, President Roosevelt was impressed enough to appoint him to the Securities and Exchange Commission in August, 1935. Back in Seattle, City Light still competitively locked horns with Puget Sound Power & Light. With Ross being appointed to such a powerful governmental position, Stone & Webster feared that he would use his advantage to make life difficult for them; but this was not the case. Ross was a man of unusual integrity and was reported as saying that, if Stone & Webster could provide power more cheaply than City Light, he would be plugging for private and not public power. (City Light finally bought out its competitor in 1951.)

One of the most powerful yet humble political figures ever to rise in the Northwest, Ross died in 1939, suddenly but peacefully, and was buried in a crypt at the foot of Ross Mountain in Newhalem. Like a Paul Bunyan of power, he had one foot in the North Cascades and the other in Seattle.

Ross also must go down in Northwest history as one of the canniest public-relations men ever to appear. When he first encountered resistance from the public about his expenditures for power, he smilingly wooed the Seattle taxpayers with Skagit Tours, which enabled thousands of people to visit the Skagit Gorge and see for themselves where their money was being spent. Ross's fine sense of the dramatic permeated the format of the tours and created a tourist attraction that was usually booked full.

Skagit Tours began in 1928, long before Diablo Dam was completed, when a civic-minded group of women, Women's City Club, wondered about the wisdom of spending so much on the Skagit Project. City Light promptly invited the group of about thirty women to see the workings, and they returned to spread approving words about the project. Within a few months regularly scheduled tours were organized, with Ed Kemoe as the first tour guide. By 1932, the setup was operating under full steam under the direction of Fran Scarvie, a handsome, athletic man who continued to squire spectators until the cancellation of the tours during World War II. Here's the way the average two-day tour went:

There were three tours a week, each handling at capacity about 600 people. Visitors drove or took a bus to Rockport, where they boarded a bright yellow steam-powered Toonerville Trolley. After a scenic ride to Newhalem, passengers disembarked about four-fifteen P.M., were assigned rooms in tents or dormitories, and were served a huge, family-style meal. Following dinner, they viewed the powerhouse by crossing a scary suspension bridge two feet wide above the Skagit River, then returned to camp for movies and other entertainment. The Forest Ranger on duty lectured about the Gorge, after which Ross addressed the group if he happened to be in camp. As darkness settled over the canyon, the party went across the river to stroll through the lighted gardens adjacent to the powerhouse. From concealed speakers came strains of inspirational music and out of trees came the songs of birds (recorded). Few thought to question why the birds sang at night. The Ladder Creek Falls were dramatically lighted with changing colored lights; and while spectators watched the water boil down the cascades toward the Skagit River, Marian Anderson could be heard singing "Ave Maria," or an organ might play "The Holy City." Filled with high romance, the tourists went back to camp for a lively dance.

They were gently awakened the following morning by the music of a special hymn, "Singing to Welcome the Pilgrims of the Night," which started softly and swelled ever-louder through speakers in each dormitory and tent. After a logger-sized breakfast, visitors boarded the trolley to Diablo; open cars permitted them to view the scenery of the Gorge. Three hundred people at a time rode the incline railway to Diablo Lake and took an excursion boat to the foot of Ross Dam. While the excursion boat nosed through the narrowest part of Diablo Lake, music came from speakers concealed high above on canyon walls. By noon the group was back in Newhalem for lunch, being serenaded by music featuring chimes from speakers on the cliffs above the camp. At departure time the tune switched to "Aloha" to waft the passengers back toward Rockport on a wave of nostalgia. It was hard to find a single cynic after the experience. For about twelve years, from May to September, thousands enjoyed the tour to the Skagit, paying a nominal fee ranging from a dollar-fifty in the beginning to six dollars in 1941. After World War II the tours were renewed, but on a one-day basis, and still operate between June and Labor Day.

15

The Rise of Ross Dam and Its Lake

The third dam of the Skagit Project, first called Ruby Dam and then Ross, was a joint venture of Seattle and the United States government, the latter contributing because the dam provided flood control for the Skagit Valley.

While the plans were on the drawing boards and the Diablo phase completed, many workers were idled but stayed on at camp because the Depression had choked off jobs. Residents of the camps, about twenty-five families at Diablo and 200 men in dormitories, made their own amusements and relied on each other in those times of trouble. There were lively Saturday night dances attended by entire families; and Diablo's small community built a swimming pool with bare hands and a few dollars. People at Diablo were isolated for almost six weeks during the winter of 1936–37 because of slides. Necessities were brought in by pack trains over the old miners' road — or what remained of it.

By the end of 1937, Seattle City Light's power systems were putting out 417,285,000 kilowatts annually, but this was still not enough, so the city launched into the Ruby (Ross) Dam project. Seattle used its own engineers to design the dam — modeled somewhat after Hoover Dam — and hired as a private consultant J. L. Savage of Denver, the most famous dam builder in the world. Credited with designing the five largest concrete dams on earth plus at least sixty others, he

130

was the consultant for the huge Burrinjuck Dam of Australia. The dam was planned in four steps: Phase One was to establish a barrier 305 feet high, completed in 1940. Phases Two and Three raised the dam to 540 feet in 1949, backing up water beyond the Canadian border. Phase Four was planned as a later raising of the dam, if power requirements became greater, and an agreement was made with British Columbia for further flooding of the upper Skagit Valley — a point presently under bitter contention by environmentalists.

Because Ross Lake was to cover a large area, timber had to be removed before the valley was flooded during Phase One. Seattle agreed to pay the U.S. government $176,619 for the 318 million board feet of timber estimated to be in the 11,820 acres to be cleared. Although City Light intensively advertised for bids, no one would tackle logging of the area immediately above the proposed dam because there was no access. All logging equipment would have had to be hoisted over the dams, and lumber taken back the same way — the method was totally impractical. Therefore, many of the trees immediately above the dam were inundated; only the tips were cut off after the lake had risen, so that boats could navigate the waters. Seattle City Light often was criticized for wasting natural resources. Some years later, deep-sea divers conceived the idea of going down with air-powered chain saws and cutting off the logs. After several dives and loss of life, the project was abandoned.

In June, 1945, a company with international connections, Decco-Walton of Everett, did sign a contract for $60,200 to remove the logs lying between elevation 1365 and 1605 feet, the present north end of the lake. Seattle City Light's loss of about $116,000 on the timber seems shocking until one examines how complicated the removal was. First, the firm had to subcontract with a Canadian firm for removal of trees at the Canadian end of the lake site. Then the two companies built about forty miles of road to the Fraser River, capable of supporting huge Kenilworth log trucks with sixteen-foot beds to handle eighty-foot logs. At the Fraser River an A-frame crane with an eighty-five-foot boom lifted off the logs and dropped them in the river, where they were boomed and transported by tug to mills — the Canadian logs to New Westminster, the American logs to Anacortes or Everett. The timber was felled, then lay unmoved until the lake rose so that it could be boomed to the north end of the lake for trucking to the Fraser.

The logging road was also used to supply a clearing camp, because, concurrent with the commercial logging, City Light contracted with Morrison-McEachern-Decco to clear the land above Ross of all scrub and slash and also the lake of debris. To provide transportation on the lake, the company had two forty-foot steel tugs, the *Steelhead* and the *City of Seattle*; also a fifty-foot wooden-hulled tug, which sank in 1958 on Ross Lake. The *Steelhead* was shipped in over the logging road on a big truck and made a crashing debut. Between the border and Devil's Creek, the truck hit soft ground and tilted, tipping the tug over into the Skagit River. It flipped completely over and landed right side up, but with a hole in its hull. Foreman Jack Sherin got a tractor to drag the boat out of the water, and the crew welded a plate over the hole. Because the motor was intact, the tug just lay in the then shallow river like a beached whale until the lake rose to float it.

The clearing camp was established on a huge log raft, 90 by 300 feet, and included a floating dry dock, comfortable bunkhouses, and an amazingly modern kitchen with such luxuries as an electric oven, dishwasher, and chrome coffee urns. The floating camp was anchored at first just above Ross Dam, a precarious and eerie home among the tops of the drowned trees, surrounded by undulating debris. To protect the new dam from pressure, a boom was stretched across the lake to catch debris. The crew started to push the debris northward, cutting and burning as they went — a project that left Ross one of the cleanest lakes in the nation.

There were freeloaders on the raft from time to time — bears. Whenever the camp was unattended, they tried to get into the stores. The more accustomed they became to seeing people, the bolder they got; and when a bear sneaked up and grabbed one man's lunch while he was working only an arm's length away, the worker quit and went back to his native New

York. Cougars attached themselves to the camp, too, sitting like big kittycats around the fringes of the work sites and watching the men unnervingly. Some of the men shared their scraps with the big cats. The mountain goats liked to have their young near the camps. Jack Sherin, foreman of the operation, said he counted as many as fifteen goats at a time on the shore of the lake. Even an occasional moose or timber wolf was spotted nearby.

Although the company used a lot of green men during the war years, the crew had its mental boundaries fixed and seldom did anyone walk off the raft into the water. Heavy drinkers were fired and even excessive card playing was frowned upon because management felt workmen would not be alert enough the following day.

The logging crew was still working to some extent on Ross Lake on March 27, 1965, when suddenly the log raft started to sway and tilt so violently that men were forced to cling to its supports. The lake broke out in big waves, two to three feet high, as if a big windstorm were in progress. At Ross Dam's powerhouse the dials on the machinery went wild for a few moments. Jack Sherin called Newhalem by radio to determine whether there was a big landslide somewhere and learned from personnel there — only a few miles away — that no tremors had been felt. The time of the incident was the same as that of the devastating Anchorage quake.

The clearing and the dam building went along concurrently. The site selected for Ross Dam was ideal — footings were placed in a deep depression thought to be the bed of an ancient waterfall. Because Diablo Lake backed up one mile beyond the site, a temporary diversion dam first had to be made to shunt upstream water around the excavation. After thunderstorms the water became so high that the barrier washed away repeatedly until engineers solved the problem by drilling holes in a series of rocks as large as two and a half cubic yards and stringing a cable through them like a necklace to hold the dam in place.

Setting up the operations camp was a difficult task. There was little flat ground between Ross and Newhalem or beyond. Materials were stacked all the way from Rockport to

Ross. In order to get one and one-half million board feet of lumber near the site for making concrete forms, a meager 40-by-150-foot spot was blasted out of the rock and lumber was stacked thirty feet high. To handle materials on the job, two immense cableways were installed, one which operated over a 2800-foot diameter and could reach almost every part of the dam, and a second one called a Joe Magee which handled concrete and other heavy materials up to ten tons.

On a narrow ledge blasted out of the cliff wall, a camp was constructed for the workers, perched on the ledges of rock with the only access by water. Life was hearty and the humor rough. When the cook had a fishing line rigged up with a bell, so that he could monitor it while he worked, the men teased him continuously by ringing it — just to watch him fly out the door, apron flapping. The cook was not amused and whipped out a revolver, threatening to shoot a few jokers.

Single men were housed two to a room, and there were a few small houses for married workers. The women in camp usually worked in the commissary or kitchen. While the company forbade drinking, it provided slot machines, permitted poker games, dice, and so on. Each man worked twelve days and was off two — not enough time to get much farther than Sedro Woolley; so, as in the heyday of the logging camps forty years earlier, the workers let off steam in the little towns of the Skagit.

Everyone grew accustomed to seeing black bears around, for they were attracted to the garbage dump. Any unoccupied building was investigated by the bears, and when a bear stole an alarm clock in one of his break-ins, the workers laughed and said he was getting ready to hibernate. The cook hot-wired garbage can lids to repel the bears because they became real pests. One worker at Diablo who shot a bear out of season had the misfortune to have the game warden come through the camp at the time, so he quickly buried the carcass behind his house. The warden heard of the illegal kill and questioned the worker.

"Oh, no," denied the man. "I don't know anything about any bear."

Just then, like retribution reaching from the grave, a big,

black, bear paw rose straight out of the ground before the fascinated eyes of the game warden and workman. Rigor mortis had set in at an inopportune moment.

Forms for the concrete were prepared at the little sawmill at the dam site, and because the dam would be built in stages, the face was cast in trapezoidal shapes to enable constructors to get a firm grip on the structure in successive stages. The finished dam has an attractive, wafflelike appearance. The heavy masses of cement required a long time to set. Coils were embedded in the mass to allow calcium chloride brine to be pumped through it for cooling. Fourteen huge refrigeration units, using freon, chilled the brine.

W. B. Wolfendale was project engineer for Ross Dam, while Charles Shevling was the on-the-job engineer during its construction. Because Seattle's wartime industry needed ever-increasing amounts of power, Phase Three followed Phase Two without interruption. The onset of war gave the tranquil settlements of Newhalem and Diablo severe cases of jitters, as it was perfectly logical to suspect that enemy bombers or saboteurs might try to blow up the dams that powered Seattle's industry. Seattle City Light went to a complete blackout the night of the Pearl Harbor attack, operating the powerhouse by flashlight. Until more definite information about the positions of Japanese aircraft carriers was obtained, a blackout continued. The generation superintendent ordered a patrol to be sure that no lights showed anywhere in Newhalem — private or public. In the unaccustomed darkness, skittish employees bumped into each other in City Light buildings.

Thomas N. Bucknell, later to become Skagit Project Manager, worked at the Skagit Project before the war, and after it was over returned to live in Diablo when the only access was by trolley. Whenever there was a good movie playing in Newhalem, several Diablo residents got together and went down on the trolley parked near Bucknell's home.

"It was just like a big party, with cocoa in thermos bottles and lots of singing on the way home," said Bucknell.

Many winter days were far from idyllic. Sometimes winds howled through the canyon at more than sixty miles per hour, while the heavy snows meant ever-present avalanche danger. One winter after reports of a huge avalanche near Ferry Bar Bridge, Bucknell and a companion went to assess the damage. As they approached the bridge, there was a loud clap of thunder, causing Bucknell to brake swiftly in alarm. The two startled men watched as a man crawled across the bridge, crawling right up to Bucknell's car. Apparently in shock, his mouth was working but no words came out. When he recovered enough to speak, he told the two men that an air blast from a second avalanche had blown him out of his snowshoes as he was crossing Ferry Bar Bridge. The force had thrown him against the bridge railing, and as he was going over the rail into the river, he instinctively hooked his arm around the rail, swinging back onto the bridge.

Bucknell and his friend walked on to inspect the devastation. The air blast had sheared off trees sixteen inches in diameter as if they had been chopped down with an axe, not from the slide, but from the concussion of the avalanche. Bits of cedar were driven into seasoned telephone poles as much as an inch. When the men walked toward the main body of the slide, they crunched along on a carpet of fir greenery up to two feet thick. The scent of pine oil in the air burned their eyes and throats.

Between Newhalem and Diablo there were seven distinct avalanche zones, areas that were vulnerable to slides that could put 300 feet of snow, eighty to ninety feet deep, on the road in seconds. No wonder prospectors in generations past had sometimes simply disappeared without trace.

The overall safety record of the Ross Dam project was good, but nature was unpredictable. For eighty days in 1943, high water poured over Ross Dam — too much water for the diversion tunnels to handle. The entire construction staff had an impromptu vacation; there was no damage to the dam but no work could be done. In 1948, as the camp residents near Ross slept or were about to retire, a killer avalanche roared down and wiped out four houses. It had been raining for two days and in the higher elevations there was wet snow. Stanley Jones was listening to the ten o'clock news when he heard a strange rattling noise, looked outside, and saw a house going by! He thought he was seeing things, but it was all too true. Jones's wife had already retired to her bedroom at the rear of the house. Her husband said later, "I yelled to her to get out. She went out the window with just her nightgown and and overcoat on and was barefoot." It was not a moment too soon for the slide pushed in the front wall of the house.

Nearby, Mr. and Mrs. J. E. Newcomb suddenly found themselves in motion, house and all, sliding down a slope toward the lake. A wall collapsed onto Mrs. Newcomb but her husband extricated her. Unfortunately Mr. Newcomb's father, who was sleeping in his bedroom, was crushed.

"That was the longest short ride I ever took," said Newcomb. "Before we stopped moving, I figgered we were going into the lake but we stopped a hundred-fifty feet short."

James A. Muir, captain of a tugboat that operated on Diablo Lake, looked up from his bed with horror to find the door bulging inward. "I tried to hold it back but the slide shoved it in on my wife. The slide drove oil drums and a refrigerator on our back porch right through the wall. Then the house tipped over. I shoved my wife out the bathroom window and followed."

Not so lucky was Mrs. Charles A. Royce when the avalanche hit her home. Her husband said, "I ran toward the bedroom where my wife was but I never got there, and I never saw her. A stove just flew at me and everything went black."

Jack Johnson was trapped for a long half-hour when he was stuck in the framework of his house as he tried to escape. His wife was injured when the side of the building collapsed. Upstairs, the slide took the roof off but only gently tipped son Roger out of his attic bed.

Coworkers, hastily pulling on clothing, probed the debris in total darkness because the slide had disrupted the power lines.

The river claimed a victim in grimly spectacular fashion in 1945, when the Ferry Bar Bridge was being reworked. While a two-man crew was working at night stacking material with a crane, the crane operator somehow overloaded the crane and the top-heavy piece of equipment toppled over into the river, making a complete revolution and landing right side up but thirty feet under water. As the crane fell, it ripped out the single row of electric lights which illuminated the bridge, leaving the remaining crewman to crawl off the partly dismantled bridge on a narrow plank suspended over the chasm. He hiked to Diablo and brought back a rescue party, but all that could be seen was the tip of the crane. Below, the Gorge powerhouse generators were stepped up to full capacity in order to take down the level of the river so a search for the man could continue, but it was raining so hard that the level did not diminish significantly for several days. The crane operator's remains never were found.

The same severe weather of 1948–49 that brought death to Ross camp also isolated the Diablo camp. Supplies grew slim and men were unable to make a path along the railroad. In order to evacuate the people, two men went over the top of the slide and closed off the tunnel at Diablo; then people were able to come through the long water tunnel and emerge at the Gorge powerhouse at Newhalem.

Ross Dam was formally accepted by Seattle City Light from the contractors on August 18, 1949, carrying a final price tag of about twenty-eight million. Concurrent with the completion of the powerhouse between 1951 and 1956, the city of Seattle commenced construction in 1954 on the High Gorge Dam to replace the original diversion dam built in 1924 — the last phase in a thirty-year power development project. Supervisor of the Design Office was C. R. Hoidal, while C. W. Cutler was the project engineer on the Skagit from 1949–59. Merritt, Chapman & Scott, a firm with a reputation for building docks and maritime buildings in the East, gained the contract for building High Gorge.

The porous nature of the terrain at the site posed an unusual problem, which was solved in an unusual way. The ground just upstream from the dam site was literally frozen solid to provide a barrier against water that had persistently seeped through into the site. Workmen drilled a series of holes four feet apart across the river channel, and in these holes installed three-foot pipe with one and one-half-inch pipe inside that. The pipe was pumped full of brine, building up a solid wall of ice and gravel across the canyon. Some of the holes were up to 200 feet deep — and the ground may still be frozen there. Unique and successful as the solution proved to be, the seepage delayed construction for a year.

As the waters backed up from High Gorge Dam, the historic trolley from Newhalem to Diablo had to be abandoned; rails and ties were removed and only the roadbed remained under water. To replace it, the contractor built the section of road from Newhalem to Diablo that comprises a portion today of the North Cascades Highway, although at the time it was a one-way road. Years later during the completion of the highway, the State's construction crews widened this road and tried to enlarge the tunnels. Because of the hardness of the walls, the idea was abandoned and the tunnels became one-way portions of the highway.

After the road was passable to Diablo, the Forest Service completed a bridge across Gorge Lake and an access to Thunder Arm of Diablo Lake for removal of timber. By bits and pieces the ramparts of the North Cascades were falling to the roadbuilders.

XXXXXXXXXXXXXXXXXXXXXXXXXXXXX

16

Roads in the Roaring Twenties

Interest in a cross-mountain road was never forgotten but merely shelved due to lack of appropriations in the early part of the century. In 1907, 1909, and 1917, a total of around $60,000 was approved but never spent. Yielding to the pressure of many citizens, the Highway Commission spent its money on north-south highways or on areas where population was increasing. Even the *Concrete Herald*, the Skagit newspaper that was later the bulwark of support for the North Cascades Highway, then opposed the road.

Pioneer Otto Klement, who had discovered gold in the upper Skagit and homesteaded in Lyman, wrote a long editorial in the *Mount Vernon Argus* in 1919, in which he reminded valley residents of the Cascade Pass Road. He mentioned the writings of Mary Roberts Rinehart in *Cosmopolitan* magazine, following her horseback trip over the pass in 1916, and of another writer who described the area for *The Saturday Evening Post*. After Klement's article appeared, urging renewal of a drive for the road, J. J. Donovan of Bellingham pledged his support.

Because industry was developing around the orchard and ranch businesses of Omak and Okanogan, those towns eagerly looked for outlets to the populous markets along Puget Sound. In 1920, at the annual meeting of the Okanogan Good Roads Association, members voted to enter politics and work for commissioners who would aggressively encourage road building — especially one across the mountains to Skagit or Whatcom county. The group asked the State organization if they could be annexed to the Western Washington Good Roads Association, instead of the Eastern Washington group, believing that Okanogan County's future was more aligned with the coast than the plateau country.

The possibility of a cross-mountain railroad came up once again in April, 1920, when Puget Sound, Spokane International Railroad announced that it would build from Spokane to Bellingham. The *Omak Chronicle* glowingly reported that the line would run from the seaport terminal of Bellingham through the "wonderfully fertile Nooksack Valley, the coal, cement and mining fields of the Mount Baker foothills, thence down the Methow Valley along the great wheat fields of the Columbia." The article noted that the railroad would "afford a route with a better grade than any from eastern Washington to Puget Sound, and a line shorter by many miles." As usual, the proponents did not specify just how they were going to accomplish these marvels.

Improvement of the roads by local commissioners turned out to be a mixed blessing in the roaring twenties, when bootleggers running liquor into the United States from Canada became a major, almost daily problem. Home-brew stills did not cause as much trouble as the international traffic. However, there were a few Skagit moonshiners (and some in Conconully) who trafficked in large enough quantities that authorities had to stop looking the other way. One of the largest operators produced mountain dew in a respectable-looking house on Ferry Street in Sedro Woolley, shipping the product to Portland and Seattle. The sheriff moved in on this operator, first sending a deputy crawling up to the getaway car to shut off its gas line, then surrounding the house and capturing the men inside.

The stills which abounded in the hill country were works of mechanical art, of shiny copper tubing and spotless tanks. It was common knowledge that a master metal craftsman in Bellingham was the supplier of much of the copperwork, but it was hard to prove him guilty because he sold only the individual pieces for a still — one at a time and for cash. When he finally was tried for conspiracy, he was freed on a technicality.

"Did you make this still?" sternly asked the judge, confronting the accused with tanks and tubing.

"No, I didn't," replied the man.

"Remember, you are in a court of law. I may be able to convict you on perjury. Now, did you make this tank?" continued the judge.

"Yes, I made the tank," came the reply.

"Did you make these coils?" queried the judge.

"Yes, I did," admitted the metalworker.

"Well, then, how can you stand there and say that you didn't make the still?" demanded the exasperated judge.

After a few minutes of thought, the canny craftsman replied, "Well, I may make tanks for people. They might use them for making ice cream or for making booze. Just because I make the tank doesn't mean I made the ice cream!"

In 1923, a big moonshine plant was discovered and destroyed at the Cokedale mines near Sedro Woolley, a substantial installation with a brick furnace, condensers and copper coils. The haul included 1300 gallons of mash and booze.

On Puget Sound, international smuggling of liquor was tied in with the boatmen who engaged in a running battle with federal agents through the complicated channels of the San Juan Islands. Skagit County fell heir to the problem when the liquor reached shore. Boats put in at lonely shores along March Point near Anacortes, or Deception Pass, where smugglers loaded their illicit cargo into waiting, fast cars, and the drivers sped toward Seattle. Along the Pacific Highway through Burlington and Mount Vernon, "cops-and-robbers" chases at high speeds were commonplace.

A fitting climax to a ribald Fourth of July celebration in Mount Vernon in 1921 was a high-speed pursuit down the main street. The sheriff had received a message from Bellingham lawmen that a car of booze runners had knocked a customs agent off his feet at the Canadian border, then fled south through Bellingham. Spying a suspicious looking seven-passenger Case auto north of Mount Vernon, the sheriff gave chase. Zigzagging through traffic, the patrol car closed the gap on the smugglers and an officer leaned out of the window and shot out the tires of the Case, causing spectators to scatter like chickens. South of town the car careened to a stop and the occupants — all Oregonians — were arrested.

A haul in April, 1922, at March Point, netted seventy cases of bonded liquor. Two weeks later, officers arrested four men armed with a rifle and two revolvers as they left Deception Pass in a touring car loaded with Canadian Scotch. During a pursuit of one bootlegger's car by the sheriff, a "moll" in the fleeing car systematically smashed bottles on the street to puncture the tires of the pursuer.

In February, 1926, a man with a guilty conscience, "Cock-eyed" Helt, came from Anacortes at terrific speed in a big Buick, lost control of the car, and went through the guard rail on the Swinomish Slough drawbridge, sailing through the air into fourteen feet of water. The drawbridge tender's two sons rescued three people from the car, but a seventeen-year-old girl drowned. Helt was arrested at the scene, when the car was raised from the water and was found to have a cache of liquor under the floorboards in a specially built compartment.

Omak and Okanogan, situated on the road south from Canada, faced the same types of problems. Through a series of backwoods trails in the foothills west of Riverside and Oroville, strange and powerful cars often were seen rushing through the night with dimmed lights. In 1921, a notorious whiskey runner, Red Prince, was shot dead at the border after first shooting at a customs man. Two years later, Okanogan County Sheriff E. J. Wilson and his deputy, B. McCauley, set a trap for a known ring operating near Riverside. Seven cars moving confidently along a road were intercepted, where-upon the passengers opened fire on the sheriff with repeating rifles. The sheriff and his deputy captured five of the men, shot one unintentionally, and chased the rest as far as the next county. In the captured cars there was not only bottled liquor but stills, coils, moonshine, and 200 gallons of mash. One of the captured men was highly indignant, declaring that he had paid "someone" in county government $500 for clear passage. The sheriff said he wasn't the one and hardheartedly put the gang behind bars.

Small-scale runners hid liquor in innocent-looking cargo such as loads of oats, potatoes, or hay, or beneath the floorboards of cars, and in ingeniously constructed special compartments. One method of operation was to bring the cargo across the border in a remote area by pack train, then transfer it to powerful cars at a rendezvous in the hills that had at least a passable dirt road. McCauley, who became sheriff of Okanogan County, had his informers. When an illicit shipment was expected, he received a cryptic note by postcard, like: "The coyotes will howl tonight." Usually the drivers were hired hands, and when jailed, their bail was paid by mysterious attorneys from large cities to the south or from Spokane. The souped-up cars were auctioned off for sizable sums, often bought by the people who really owned them, and sometimes appearing on the auction block more than once.

Sheriff Bernard McCauley was a legendary western lawman, fearless, totally honest, and a little reckless. On one occasion he and two deputies intercepted a convoy of runners in a lonely spot near Riverside and found that — instead of the expected two cars — there were eight. When McCauley and his deputies swung onto the highway after the convoy, the chase proceeded through Riverside, Omak, and Okanogan at a searing pace. At Okanogan the bootleggers swerved across a bridge to a county road east of the river known as the Corkscrews — a steep and narrow road that led up a canyon and onto the Colville Reservation. In a convoy the strategy of runners was to sacrifice the last car and permit the rest to escape; so on the narrow road the last car slowed to a crawl to block McCauley, but the driver didn't reckon with the sheriff's freewheeling style. McCauley gunned his engine, sent his car up on the steep inside bank of the road, and deliberately sideswiped the runner's car off the road, where it rolled over once and stopped. He repeated the carnage until all eight cars were off the road. Miraculously none of the runners were hurt but certainly they were impressed and came out of their cars with hands high.

Not all the smugglers were passive. In 1931, a car belonging to Jack McCauley, brother of the sheriff, was dynamited into bits as it stood in front of his home in Twisp. So violent was the explosion that bits of the vehicle were blown into trees and onto nearby rooftops. The blast apparently was intended for Bernard, not Jack.

Despite such misuse of the good roads, the North Cascadians organized as the Cascade Pass Highway Pilgrims to promote a cross-mountain highway. Leadership of the group on the west side included: David McIntyre, David Donnelly, Albert Mosier, Charles Gable, Burt Moody, Tom Chambers; and on the east: Senator Bolinger, Harry Kerr, Leonard Therriault, Les Holloway, and Irvin Stokes. The Pilgrims gained the support of Governor Roland Hartley and through his influence the legislature appropriated $70,000 in 1924 for construction between Marblemount and the summit of Cascade Pass. Once again, the road which had been started in 1896 was improved for five and one-half miles, but it began and ended nowhere because there was no bridge across the Skagit River from the valley highway. Although the State provided $150,000 in 1927, plus another $35,000 for such a bridge if Skagit County provided matching funds, nothing happened because Skagit had no funds. Worse yet, the new Pacific Highway Bridge (north-south highway) across the river near Mount Vernon became dangerously decrepit and had to be replaced. Because Skagit was unable to do the job, the State used $70,000 of its $150,000 Cascade Pass appropriation on the Mount Vernon Bridge. The Cascade Pass road work was halted until a $200,000 appropriation in 1929 made construction of the Marblemount Bridge possible.

Boosters of the Cascade Pass idea continued to exert pressure on politicians and the media. They tried to interest Seattleites by proposing a loop highway for tourists from Lake Chelan to the Skagit Valley and down to Seattle. But Seattle was wooed only to the extent of proposing that the Forest Service build such a road — since much of the right-of-way was on government land. Elected officials and governmental agencies found it hard to make definite commitments because the various towns of the North Cascades could not agree on a route. In 1924, a major part of Twisp had burned down, and to encourage mining business to locate in Twisp, the Commercial Club suggested a cross-mountain road or partial crossing via Azurite Pass, where there was mining interest.

Skagit citizens became split into two factions — one led by McIntyre for Cascade Pass, the other by Van Horn's Richard Buller for a Slate Creek-Hart's Pass route. Whatcom County favored the latter route because much of it would be within its boundaries. Winthrop always favored the Hart's Pass route because it was the closest town to Hart's Pass, and when the present North Cascades Highway route was proposed, Winthrop favored it for the same reason. The Skagit Chamber of Commerce (mostly lower valley residents) wanted the Cascade Highway to run from Spokane to Port Townsend on the Olympic Peninsula, making the unbuilt Deception Pass Bridge a part of the project to connect Whidbey Island with the mainland. No wonder, then, that little was accomplished by any group.

The Forest Service and Seattle City Light cooperated in improving the road from Rockport to Diablo Dam, because City Light used trucks and Charles H. Park, forestry supervisor of the Forest Service, wanted a road "so that motor tourists may have a better chance to view the beauties of the upper Skagit." At the urging of Duncan McKay of the Forest Service, a tract of towering virgin cedar was also preserved along the highway as Rockport State Park.

The newly built Baker River Bridge along the Skagit Valley Highway was the scene of a labor showdown in 1924 between the I.W.W. or "wobblies" and the town of Concrete. On October 16, 500 men left their jobs at the Baker River Dam, some of them members of the union. The town coped with the milling men until about November 1, when I.W.W. pickets were imported from Seattle. According to the accounts of Concrete residents, these men were unruly and insulting, aggravating the residents in myriads of ways. The small town had an aging, part-time mayor, Dan Dillard, who stood on the bridge one day watching logs floating on the river below, when pickets allegedly accosted him, taunted him, and roughed him up. This so enraged the citizens that Sheriff C. R. Conn and deputies marched into the crowd collecting at the bridge and repeated an earlier warning that only two pickets were allowed on the bridge at one time. When the I.W.W. men still did not move, the deputies (most pressed into service that day) moved through the group, rounding up most of the pickets. The outsiders were marched through town — suffering the angry jeers of the natives — and loaded onto trucks for transportation out of the county.

Left to themselves, local workers (I.W.W. and uncommitted) ironed out their differences with the management within two days. Nine men were held in the county jail because they were foreigners without passports. One of these men offered the chilling information that, during the entire incident at the bridge, armed wobblies had been hiding with rifles trained on the lawmen. The spokesman added that, because such a large force of deputies appeared, they had not opened fire. The otherwise bloodless incident could have been a massacre.

Starting in 1926, the Cascade Pass Pilgrims scheduled annual pilgrimages by foot or horseback to the top of Cascade Pass, where influential east- and westsiders met to publicize the proposed road.

During the 1929 pilgrimage the eastsiders boarded a chartered barge tied between two boats on Lake Chelan, the *Comanche* and the *Mohawk*. A hired orchestra was aboard and everyone was in a holiday mood, dancing and talking. Two hours later the barge started to sink so rapidly that it was beached at Safety Harbor to be pumped out and repaired. Undisturbed by the incident, some of the passengers and the band went ashore to continue dancing, while others went swimming or brought out picnic lunches. Eventually the party arrived at Stehekin, allowing forty-eight people to hike over the pass and on to Marblemount for the dedication of the Marblemount Bridge, where Governor Hartley and Samuel Hume, director of highways, spoke.

In that year of 1929, the stock-market collapse effectively severed the financial pipeline to the Cascade Pass Road. Only a few road appropriations could be made for several years. Also, in the Depression-torn years of the thirties, Clarence Martin, the new governor, was not particularly in favor of the Cascade Pass Highway. He did, however, assist Okanogan County generously by sanctioning improvements on the road between Omak and Okanogan, the construction of a new bridge at Pateros, and work on the highway between Winthrop and Twisp. Each of these segments of road eventually became part of the completed North Cascades Highway.

17

There Is Gold in the Mountains

High on a mountain above Slate and Canyon creeks, two gold mines, thought to be part of the same deposit, became the focal point for all the road-building propaganda of the 1930s. Charles and Hazard Ballard, prospectors who had come over the old Colockum Trail from Ellensburg in 1886 and worked in Conconully and the Slate Creek areas, discovered the Azurite Mine in 1916 and the Gold Hill in 1917, on opposite sides of the same 5,400-foot ridge. Charles took possession of the Azurite and Hazard the Gold Hill, but neither was able to mine seriously until Charles accumulated some capital in 1929, with which to develop the mining property. To house his men Charles Ballard built a bunkhouse, as well as a smithy shop, partly into the mountainside for protection against avalanches. In winter the only sign of its existence was the smoke issuing through the snow from the chimney.

Because it was impossible to transport equipment by trail from Newhalem, Ballard had to improve Hart's Pass Road at his own expense and obtain his machinery and supplies from Seattle by a roundabout route through the Methow. Too large to be carried by a single packhorse, the flywheels for the two diesel compressors, which were nine feet in diameter, were cast in three sections and bolted together at the Azurite camp. After assembly, Ballard planned to run one compressor each week and shut down the other for servicing, but during the first week of the mine's operation a compressor threw a rod through its engine. Because it was winter, a repairman summoned from the Chicago Pneumatic Company of Pennsylvania had to travel to the mine on snowshoes from Mazama and transport his tools and personal gear by dog sled. Thereafter, the mine owner never dared run either compressor at full capacity, fearing further repairs.

Before the installation of a $20,000 Mace Smelter to process ore in 1932, the mine used a primitive, homemade rock crusher. In a large wooden tank lined with rocks at the bottom, ore-bearing rock was smashed by a weighted, revolving wooden wheel powered by water pressure. After the rock was crushed, a cyanide solution added to it caused the base metals to dissolve; thereafter, when zinc shavings were put into the solution, the gold alone settled to the bottom of the tank for removal. According to Gordon Bainter, a Blaine, Washington, man who walked 150 miles to go to work for the Azurite in 1932, the Mace Smelter ran only one season. Because the ore being mined had an unusually high iron content, the methods used in the Mace Smelter failed to separate out the gold properly.

When the mine began full-scale operations, Azurite managers turned to the transportation firm of Stonebreaker Brothers and Johnson of Orofino, Idaho, for the difficult job of supplying their needs. With a brave but awkward slogan, "If you want to move the Woolworth Building, we'll move that where you want it," Stonebreaker was undaunted by the adverse conditions on the Hart's Pass Road. To carry materials from Hart's Pass Road up Azurite Mountain to the mine, Stonebreaker developed narrow-gauge wagons and sleds which were equipped with special tracks in a Twisp garage. During dry summer weather supplies were hauled to the junction of the Azurite trail and Hart's Pass Road with five special trucks obtained from International Harvester — odd-looking vehicles with no fenders and extra-narrow axles. In winter all supplies were moved by dog teams and sleds, handled by Ed Kikendall and his brother, Chuck. Ed claimed he had "clumb trees on skis" and had run a trap line in the mountains since he was eight years old. Later, he and Charlie Biart lived entire winter seasons in the wilderness, trapping lynx, marten, fox, and weasel, shooting rabbits and squirrels for food, and wearing the same clothes for months at a time — wool underwear, about four shirts, and leather-topped rubber boots with skis strapped on.

The dogs were mostly cross-breds heavily laced with husky blood. The lead dog was a beautiful, pure white Siberian husky with pale, milky-blue eyes — an animal reportedly worth more than $1500. Kikendall said he was the safest dog of the teams to be around, but that he frightened people with his odd eyes. Although he loved attention, he was too proud to beg and just sat, looked at people, and waited for them to come to him.

Stonebreaker had a contract with Ballard's Azurite Mining Company which specified four trips monthly to the mine, each with a payload of at least eighty pounds. If the dogs couldn't get in, the men were required to backpack that same amount of supplies to the Azurite. A round trip could take as little as two days or a whole week, depending on the weather. To make sure they fulfilled the contract, the Kikendalls set out once every week to satisfy their four-trip requirement. In addition to vital mining supplies and food, the teams carried mail and light personal items for the crew. Because sound carried long distances in the clear mountain air, miners heard the barking, belled teams long before they arrived.

Usually the teams went up the shorter but steeper Azurite Pass out of the Methow Valley, rather than Hart's Pass. The first time Kikendall and his brother left for the Azurite, a sudden storm struck, forcing them to hole up in a makeshift cave made by spreading a big tarpaulin over a bunch of brush. While the wind howled and snow piled up, the Kikendalls and teams spent two snug days together.

"The dogs sat restlessly or crossly snapped at each other," commented Ed. "After two days of men and dogs living that close, the air got pretty thick in there."

When the Azurite manager radioed to Winthrop that the dog team had not arrived, the townspeople, many of whom had scoffed at the idea of using dogs in the first place, became concerned about the safety of the Kikendalls. However, one man pointed out that Ed was a veteran mountain man, that "if a Kikendall is lost up there in the mountains, then it's too tough for me!" When the storm abated and the teams were able to go on to the Azurite, they were greeted with great relief.

The Depression hit the Methow Valley hard. Otto Wagner's lumber mill and box factory on the Loup Loup Road — one of the few industries in the area — burned to the ground in August, 1931, adding to the scarcity of employment until he relocated in Twisp. An overheated motor on the main saw at the Wagner mill set off the fire on a dry, windy day. The flames enveloped the box factory and spread down the narrow, brush-covered canyon. Employees barely escaped with their lives. Kathryn Wagner, who was working as a cook's helper at the time, recalled that one woman speeding from the fire got out and doused a blazing mattress strapped to the top of her car with a can of milk — the only liquid she had. Currents created by the fire were so great that steel roofs of the mill buildings were carried through the air. Consuming property estimated to be worth $250,000, the fire continued down the canyon to destroy a full mile of wooden flume that provided an auxiliary water supply from Wagner's mill pond for the Boston-Okanogan Orchards on the Columbia.

Considering the jobs that were being created by the operation of the Azurite Mine, Congressman E. F. Banker of the Methow Valley worked hard in the legislature to obtain a road to the coast — a project he had been interested in as a "Pilgrim." In 1932 he wangled a special appropriation of $15,000 to finance a new survey for such a highway. Ivan "Ike" Munson, a district location engineer, moved into the valley on Memorial Day with a crew of more than 30 men including a cook and packers, many of them students employed for the summer months. Munson's crew set up its first camp at Early Winters Creek, the end of the Methow Valley Road. From there the crew worked five miles each way, taking levels and contours. As soon as each ten-mile segment was completed, the camp was advanced and the process repeated.

Munson's orders were to survey a proposed route up Early Winters Creek as far as Washington Pass, then proceed down

State Creek to its junction with Bridge Creek. At Cascade Pass the feasibility of a tunnel was to be explored. However, while Munson was working in the mountains, he investigated Rainy Pass as an alternate route and was so impressed with its possibilities that he filed a strong recommendation that the highway be built over Rainy Pass (as it was later). After looking at Cascade Pass, Munson was gloomy about the idea of building a road over its steep south face, where there were such steep cliffs that his surveyors swung on ropes to complete their work in places. Often they were able to progress only 500 to 600 feet a day.

During the same summer, Sam Humes, state director of highways, told highway boosters in Mount Vernon in August that the State intended to let bids on the Cascade Pass Road, using the $200,000 appropriation made in 1929. He added that, in order for the federal government to provide matching funds, such a road must be declared a primary road and advised supporters to work toward that classification. But the Depression-strained budgets did not allow anything to progress.

Because road and trail building was a basic part of relief programs, however, the Depression turned out to be good for the development of the North Cascades. During the summer of 1933, 200 young men in the Civilian Conservation Corps built 37 miles of truck roads and maintained 223 miles of other roads on Forest Service land near Marblemount and Concrete, while young men in a camp on Robinson Creek improved the Hart's Pass Road. The latter were all young black men from New York and New Jersey who had never been in the wilderness. They were taken into the hearts of the Methow Valley residents, and when their baseball team beat all the other CCC camp teams for the region, local people cheered them on like hometown boys.

Road builders in the mountains fought a constant battle with bad weather, which seemed even worse in 1933. After heavy summer rainstorms caused numerous landslides all along the Skagit Valley Road, a huge mass of dirt came down in November east of Concrete to cover both the road and the railroad. Continued rains during the following weeks triggered new slides above that point, closed all roads, and sent the Skagit River flooding over the dikes of the lower Skagit. To repair the widespread damage, Governor Martin allotted $44,950 of the State's unemployment emergency funds in 1934 for work on the road from Anacortes to Marblemount, adding $245,000 for construction of the Deception Pass Bridge from Fidalgo Island to Whidbey. The CCC camp based near Marblemount received orders to rebuild the old road to Newhalem, scenic but almost impassable.

Rain in the valleys meant snow in the mountains. Earl Olds and Raleigh Sutherland of the small Flying Cloud Mine near the Azurite tried to go to the mine in January, 1934. Olds slipped while trying to cross a snowslide at the infamous Dead Horse Point and plummeted down the mountainside, alternately tumbling over and dropping down sheer portions of the almost vertical bank. Miraculously he wound up in a snowbank at the bottom unhurt, luckier than the pack train of decades earlier that had given the precipitous point its name.

Despite the problems of operating at high altitude, the Azurite Mine did yield worthwhile amounts of ore, encouraging the Tacoma Smelter to consider opening a 500-ton smelter at Pateros. In January, 1934, Charles Ballard announced that American Smelting & Refining Company, part of the vast Guggenheim Syndicate, was interested in leasing the Azurite on a fifty-fifty basis and would invest large amounts of capital. He added that American Smelting would build a hundred-ton reduction plant at the mine site, and that a road would be built from the Azurite to Diablo Dam to connect with the Skagit Valley Road.

After struggling for twenty years to develop the mine, Charles Ballard died of pneumonia in December at the age of seventy-five, before he could realize his dream. His wife, Anne, a capable businesswoman, became the president of Azurite Mining company and actively shared in the direction of the firm. Within a month of his brother's death, Hazard Ballard sold his Gold Hill Mine to a group of Alaskan investors and joined the Azurite operations as manager.

Congressman Fred Martin from the Skagit Valley agreed

with his colleagues that a cross-Cascades highway was dead unless it could be shown that there was greater employment in the mines. At last, here was a big mining effort — the Azurite, backed by and in partnership with a huge national concern, American Smelting. Not only that, but the mine's new owner actually stated that the company would help to build a road through the mountains. Road boosters and those in the political arena turned their efforts toward a routing from Diablo to the Azurite, and on over Hart's Pass Road.

Meanwhile, further lands were being removed from commercial development in the North Cascades, and wilderness proponents lobbied against roads. As the result of a walk over Cascade Pass in 1930, famed conservationist Bob Marshall recommended that the area from Cascade Pass to Ruby Creek be made into a wilderness area. In March, 1931, the United States did set aside 172,800 acres of the Mount Baker National Forest as the Whatcom Primitive Area (not the area indicated by Marshall), ranging from the Canadian border to Mount Watson and Diobsud Buttes. In September, 1934, the North Cascades Primitive Area of 801,000 acres was created, a wilderness larger than the entire state of Rhode Island. The battle between developers and conservationists would continue to escalate.

The new owners of Hazard Ballard's Gold Hill Mine were more vociferous than American Smelting in their efforts to get a road built to Azurite Mountain. On March 14, 1935, at their instigation, a group of prospectors, miners, and businessmen met and organized the Northwest Prospectors & Miners Association. The group declared that there was greater mineral wealth within a sixty-mile radius of Marblemount than in all of British Columbia, and that the only element lacking was roads. Delegates from the association traveled to Bellingham to propose to county officials that a county road be built from Ruby to a point near Azurite Mine, with the help of Azurite and Gold Hill mines. Ore would then be transported from Azurite Mountain by aerial tram to trucks for shipment via the Skagit. Mr. Pulver of Gold Hill stated that his firm had $80,000 worth of machinery ready to move onto its mining site.

Again Depression measures helped the road efforts. WERA (Washington Emergency Relief Association) verified that building roads into a mining district was an ideal way of using WERA money. Engineer C. E. Phoenix and a Whatcom County crew moved in to survey. Upon receipt of the survey report, the commissioners proposed to build a ten-foot road and seek funds as a WPA project. With such keen interest in the Azurite project, Cascade Pass Road was eclipsed and suggestions to make the latter a mine-to-market road were postponed. Because the proposed Azurite road would connect with the existing Hart's Pass artery, Okanogan County businesses chimed in with approvals. Biles-Coleman of Omak was making consumer products such as radio cabinets and store shelving, while Omak Evaporator Company, with a staff of one hundred, was marketing dried fruits. Both welcomed additional coastal access.

Despite unusually hazardous winter conditions, American Smelting & Refining continued to move equipment and supplies into the Azurite Mine during 1934–35, over the Hart's Pass approach. Avalanche danger became extreme when a large snowpack on the ground froze with an icy crust during thirty-eight-degrees-below-zero weather, followed by a second snowfall, which piled up twelve to fourteen feet of snow on top of the slippery base.

At the Azurite the extreme cold had frozen the water in the cookhouse, and Charlie Graves, the cook, was forced to chop a hole in a nearby stream to carry water. As he was fetching water one day, a slide swept down and buried him. No one missed him at first, but later, when the crew could not find him, they guessed correctly that he might be under the snow. Hastily they shoveled the snow aside, releasing the half-suffocated man, unhurt but sputtering.

Others were not so lucky that terrible winter. Repeatedly avalanches claimed the lives of men living in isolated mountain cabins. Two trappers living at a cabin on Trout Creek (near Slate Creek) usually came to Mazama every week to get their mail. When they had not appeared for several weeks, a search party snowshoed to their camp and found the men dead in their sleeping bags, the wrecked cabin half-buried by a snowslide.

An old man, Johnny Young, lived alone about four miles from the Azurite on Mill Creek, acting as caretaker for a small mine. The Azurite personnel kept an eye on the eighty-year-old Young and, shortly after the big slide, Gordon Bainter and Dick Horn traveled to Young's camp to bring him some ham and bacon. They found Young's cabin smashed in, a half-eaten meal still on the table and dirty dishes and pans on the stove, indicating that Young had left abruptly. Following Young's erratic trail about two miles from the cabin toward Slate Creek, Bainter and Horn found Johnny lying on his back, his feet still in skis. He had been dead for several days and was bitten around the neck and head, probably by a coyote. The two men tried to carry the frozen corpse to a Slate Creek cabin. Unable to reach it because of another slide, they tied old Johnny Young high up in a tree out of reach of wild animals. Two weeks later the coroner and undertaker from Winthrop showshoed in to give him a decent burial.

At Wallgren, a little post office established in the Slate Creek area by Whatcom County, Jimmy Hunter and his wife, along with a second couple, were acting as caretakers of the old Mammoth Mine. During the big January storm no one dared to go to the nearby creek to draw water because of snowslides. Tired of drinking flat-tasting melted snow, Hunter grabbed a pail one day and went to the creek just as a big slide came down, killing him with the concussion. (Mountain man Kikendall said that a person looks normal if he dies from concussion, but his face turns black if he suffocates in a slide.)

Throughout the treacherous winters the Azurite miners worked, supplied by the Kikendall dog teams. During the summer of 1936 the trucks brought in, piece by piece, a one-hundred-ton ball mill, along with a sophisticated cyanide plant, to extract the gold. At the end of the extractor's cycle, a vacuum machine with canvas bags sucked out the gold dust; every two or three weeks the bags were burned, melting the gold, which ran into molds. The cone-shaped bricks were transported to the Farmers State Bank at Winthrop for storage until the time of shipment to the Tacoma Smelter. George Dibble, Winthrop bank manager, said there was never a robbery of the lone trucks or dog teams because the gold was transported in a semirefined state, which was not particularly salable.

While the Azurite was the only mine that took out significant quantities of gold, there were others operating. One of the larger companies was the New Light Mine, which brought in a fifty-ton mill in 1936 and planned to increase its output to 200 tons. During July the New Light received six to eight truckloads of equipment per day.

With all this freight business going through the Methow Valley, Skagit Valley redoubled its efforts to get the Azurite road in from Diablo and Ruby and obtain the revenue for Skagit towns. As in past promotions, its efforts were futile. Two organizations, in particular, vied for support — the Tillicum Club and the old Cascade Pass Highway Association, renamed "Cascades Route 2 Cross-State Highway Association." Led by Richard Buller of Van Horn, the Tillicum Club favored development of the Skagit Valley road before the cross-mountain artery. Advocating that a cross-mountain road by any route be given primary consideration was the Cascade Pass group under its president, David McIntyre of Sedro Woolley. To publicize the road effort, Concrete held its first annual "Cascade Days" in August, 1936, with a parade, queen, and carnival.

Because the Azurite road was mostly in Whatcom County, a delegation from Bellingham went all the way over the proposed routing on horseback to the Azurite, where they found sixty men at work. Among the group were representatives of the Forest Service, A. B. Culmer, secretary of the Bellingham Chamber of Commerce, and John Pierce, chairman of the Chamber's Mining Committee. Impressed by the intense activity at the Azurite, the investigators concluded that a mine-to-market road was highly desirable and swung into high gear promoting it thereafter. In fact, John Pierce worked for a cross-mountain highway until his death in 1971, one year before its completion.

In order to get funds, it was vitally important to get the road declared a primary highway. Congressman Fred Martin introduced a bill in the State House of Representatives in January, 1937, to establish a road from Anacortes to the Methow Valley (not specifying any route) as Primary Highway No. 24. Although conflicting bills were introduced by two other factions, Martin's bill was approved. Only then was it discovered that the highway had been a primary road all along! Its status as State Highway No. 1, dating back to the 1893–1897 effort, or the Cascade Pass Road, had never been repealed.

Just because the approval had been made did not mean that the road was launched. Neither the weather, economic conditions, nor political machinations cooperated.

Again cold weather and heavy snows plagued the North Cascades during the winter of 1936–37. In February, Seattle City Light's train had just left Rockport for Newhalem, when a slide thundered down across the tracks ahead. While the steam locomotive labored slowly backwards toward Rockport, a second slide blocked its escape. Crews worked from both directions to free the train and its marooned passengers. Six miles up on the Cascade Pass Road a one-hundred-foot bridge that soared over a thirty-five-foot canyon was wiped out. On the old Morovits Ranch above Baker Lake the snow froze onto the roofs of the buildings and flattened them. The same conditions leveled the remaining structures of the unfortunate Baker Hatchery. An old trapper, Mathew Thomas, disappeared from his trap line near Lake Illabot in the Skagit Valley.

On January 16 of this terrible winter, news came from Azurite Mine that Fred White, a college boy working temporarily at the mine, had become ill with what appeared to be appendicitis. Kikendall had just left the mine and had offered to take the boy out, but the latter thought he was all right. When Ed and his team got partway to Winthrop a day and a half later, he met Sumner ("Stoney") Stonebreaker mushing uphill with Doctor Murdock on a sled pulled by four borrowed dogs. Murdock transferred to Kikendall's rig and the team went back into the blizzard, stopping only four hours to rest en route, arriving at the mine about noon the next day.

Young White, son of a Tacoma smelter engineer, was indeed ill. News of the emergency crackled out onto the national wire services, and the whole country followed the drama being enacted high in the North Cascades. Hearing over the radio that a surgical nurse was needed to enable Doctor Murdock to operate at the mine, a nurse from San Francisco phoned Winthrop to say that she was leaving for the Methow immediately and would parachute into the mine. Astonished Azurite officials declined her offer, but the woman flew to the Methow Valley anyway.

At the mine Murdock decided against making the operation, because of the high altitude and primitive operating conditions. Hoping to reach the hospital in time to save White, Murdock ordered the stricken man lashed securely to a dog sled. Weary Ed Kikendall set out toward Winthrop immediately with his tiring team, the sled carrying both White and Doctor Murdock. Several miners who volunteered to accompany the group suffered from exposure, and wound up needing help themselves.

When the dogs reached Robinson Creek, they were met by nationally known Idaho dog-sled driver Earl Kimball, and a racing dog team, which transported Fred White and Doctor Murdock eight more miles to a waiting State Patrol car. Sirens screaming, the car sped to the Okanogan Hospital via Pateros, a one-hundred-mile trip instead of fifty because the more direct Loup Loup Road was blocked by heavy snow. By the time Murdock finally performed the operation, it was too late. The appendix had already ruptured and the boy lived to say only a few words. Because it had been as cold as twenty degrees below zero above Robinson Creek and Murdock was an elderly man, he, too, became severely ill with pneumonia and barely lived.

Only forty-five days later, a second man became ill with symptoms similar to White's. This time the mine supervisor drafted fifteen men to start out of the mountains with stricken Howard James, while the radio summoned the Kikendall teams. Ten men walked out in front as "dogs" and the others surrounded the toboggan to guide it. At one point the mountain's slope was so steep that the men had to balance the toboggan on edge to keep it somewhat level. It got out of control and plummeted over a precipice, swinging in midair from the guide ropes. Only the swift thinking of the rescuers saved James; when the toboggan began to slide away, they immediately sat down in their tracks, braced themselves against the expected jolt, and held onto the ropes. Recovering their shaken patient, the miners met the dog team at Cady Cabin near Cady Pass, where they handed James over to Kikendall. Although weakened by pain and exposure, the man did make it to the hospital and survived his operation for an infected appendix. A courageous fellow, he was back at the Azurite within a month.

Three weeks later, on April 10, Chris Weppler also came down with symptoms of appendicitis at the Azurite. Again the dog team had just left for the valley — an instant replay of a nightmare. Kikendall said that slides were growling everywhere in the spring rains, so he had gone into the mine and back out as swiftly as possible. Just as he started to feed his dogs, the telephone rang. His brother Chuck answered and came out of the cabin, yelling,

"Don't feed the dogs. We've got to go back right away."

Attaching a double team to one sled, Ed and Chuck set a killing pace as far as Carlson's Cabin, partway to the mine, where Chuck stayed to get some rest. Ed went on to meet the men from the Azurite coming down with Weppler, who had fought snowslides, freezing rain, snow, and wind to bring him as far as possible. At Carlson Cabin, Chuck rejoined Ed and took over the arduous job of guiding the sled. Desperately tired now, the dogs struggled on to Dead Horse Point — the end of the snow, the beginning of bare road. Fresh men were supposed to be waiting, but no one was there. Chuck took the dogs down the trail, while Ed remained with Chris Weppler until help came. Ed explained: "We had to keep the dogs moving because if they had been allowed to stop in that state of fatigue, they would have stiffened up and we wouldn't have been able to move them home."

After the frantic pace down the mountainside, the hours of waiting in silence seemed interminable. Ed concluded that there must have been some misunderstanding about the rendezvous point. If Weppler did have appendicitis, every moment that passed could be critical. Finally Ed asked Chris if he could walk and supported him down to Robinson Creek, where the rescuers were waiting to take Weppler to Leavenworth. He survived the operation — though at the time of surgery doctors predicted he was only about an hour from death.

The dogs were too tired to eat, even though they had been fed nothing for two days. Kikendall said, "It was the nearest I ever was to absolute exhaustion. I slept for two days and nights before waking up. The mailman came by, saw Chuck and I asleep and determined that we indeed were not dead or anything. So he just fed the dogs for us and let us sleep."

The snowslides of the winter of 1936–37 continued to come through the Azurite installation. Only the bunkhouse, mill and offices were fairly safe because they were built into the hillside with snow sheds over them. On one occasion the slides buried the structures completely but did not damage them. However, a huge snowslide roared down the mountain and crashed into the ore bin, then carried it on farther to smash the aerial tram leading to the road. Because there was no other way to get replacement cable for the tram into the site, two reels were put on a Ford tri-motor plane, and the aircraft dropped the reels onto the site from its cargo door — undoubtedly one of the first such drops in the history of mining or aviation.

In spite of its problems, the Azurite continued to produce continuously until 1939, reportedly netting almost one million dollars in gold and silver while under lease to American Smelting & Refining. At this time the Azurite Gold Company engaged a testing laboratory to do further analysis on the site before renewing the lease. When the lab report was unfavorable, Azurite and ASARCO suspended operations and the latter removed its equipment.

All during the period that the Azurite was operating, the Prospectors & Miners Association and other groups continued to work for the completion of at least one mining road. Whatcom County tried to provide an access from the west by putting a crew of forty men into a Slate Mountain camp to construct a county road to Diablo, but did not complete it before the Azurite and Gold Hill mines ceased operations.

On July 1, 1937, the *Seattle Star* announced a contest with prizes for the best letters stating why the Cascade Pass Highway should or should not be built. It seemed, though, that the editors had a definite bias. The newspaper itself proposed arguments against the road — that it would destroy natural wilderness, substituting soda-pop stands and billboards, and that the expense was not justified because there already were three good pass roads in Stevens, Snoqualmie and Chinook. The *Star*'s competitor, the *Seattle Post-Intelligencer*, drily commented that the road up the Skagit Valley was the world's worst thoroughfare, lending an offhanded "for" vote.

The state and federal governments also were changeable in their attitudes toward roads in the North Cascades. In August, 1937, the Federal Bureau of Public Roads allocated $60,000 to resurface the Loup Loup Road (a fragment of today's completed North Cascades Hghway), announcing that it was ready to match funds with the State any time the latter decided to start construction on the cross-mountain highway. By December, President Roosevelt curtailed all federal aid for highway construction.

The State of Washington spent more than a half-million dollars to improve the Methow Valley road, eventually a segment of the North Cascades Highway, but declined to spend any further money on a cross-mountain road until it completed Stevens and White Pass roads. Lacey Murrow expressed his doubts about the wisdom of a Cascade Pass routing as well, because thirty-four miles of the road would be above 3,500-foot elevation. Besides that, the proposed road would cross two passes, Cascade at 5,392 feet and Twisp at 6,066 feet, which would make it difficult to keep open more than half of the year. The future of the cross-mountain road seemed tenuous.

In March, 1938, a heavy rainstorm in the Loup Loup area sent floodwaters into Wagner's old millpond, bursting the dam and sending a torrent down toward the little town of

Malott. It was not a very large flood, but trees and timbers from the burned-out Wagner mill were carried downstream to create a temporary dam above the town. Too late, a rancher on horseback galloped into town to warn the residents to flee. The water broke through the makeshift barrier and rushed down upon Malott, destroying several homes and businesses. Mrs. Sidney Denton got her six children out of the house, but the structure floated away all in one piece into the Okanogan River and broke up. George Phillips, owner of the quaintly spelled Seatle's Store, scoffed that "the little old creek couldn't do much damage," but the creek hit the store with such force that it drove a log right through a window. The store began to fill up with water inside, and a clerk standing on the counter simply threw open a door on the downstream side to let the water flow on through. Years later a carpenter re-modeling Hand's Store found mud still jammed inside the door frames. The water washed down two streets of Malott and spread out as it ran into the river.

That same year the hamlet of Concrete was plummeted into national headlines by an amused press corps. On a rainy fall evening half the townspeople were engrossed in a radio drama, *War of the Worlds*, by H. G. Wells, about Martians who were invading the earth. The presentation was so realistic that, just as the radio announcer announced hysterically, "The Martians have landed," residents who tuned in late believed the announcement was a news broadcast. Amplifying the listeners' alarm, a short at Concrete's substation caused the lights to go out all over town. With radio and lights off, several citizens believed that the Martians had truly landed. Within minutes the streets were filled with people — some puzzled, some frightened, some running along half-dressed or in night clothes. Through pouring rain others left their cars running at the curb and fled blindly. The same reaction occurred here and there nationally, but in Concrete the coincidence of the power blackout at the crucial moment amplified the public's reaction. While embarrassed Concrete residents squirmed, their story was reported in national publications.

18

Publicity and Political Pressure Get Results

Despite its lack of interest in a cross-mountain highway, the State looked favorably on the concept of mine-to-market roads, local arteries to permit exploitation of mineral and timber resources. In 1939, Fred Martin, senator from Skagit County, spearheaded a bill appropriating $100,000 for such a road toward Cascade Pass, with matching funds to be furnished by the county. Influencing the legislature's approval was the depressed state of Skagit's lumber industry, where severe competition from Canadian mills had caused many shingle mills to close. In fact, local shingle workers prepared messages of protest to President Roosevelt, written on shingles:

> This shingle was made by tax-paying American citizens in the United States, who contribute to all taxes of American government. It was not made by low-paid Oriental labor in Canada! To furnish steady employment to the men who made this shingle, and to the men who produce the logs, and keep them off the WPA or Government relief, enact and enforce a quota on imported shingles equal to 25% of our consumption.

Depression-torn Skagit County had no matching funds with which to build the mine-to-market road, so Martin wrested from the Senate Roads and Bridges Committee an agreement to accept the county's donation of equipment, in lieu of cash. However, two weeks later, Governor Langlie

165

killed the proposed appropriation as unnecessary and vetoed the entire $250,000 mine-to-market bill.

As war clouds gathered in Europe, a major breakthrough in the stalemate about routings across the North Cascades transpired in 1940 during a meeting of Regional Forest Service officials in Portland. L. D. Holloway persuaded other boosters to join with Forest Service and Highway Department personnel in scrapping forever the Cascade Pass Highway idea and agreeing on a route across Washington and Rainy passes — that of today's completed highway. Because of World War II and the urgent recovery measures required afterwards, nothing was done about a cross-mountain road until 1953. Progress that had been made on segments of the highway from Omak to Sedro Woolley was set back by lack of maintenance and by the big flood of the Methow River in 1948.

During the last week of May the weather turned very warm, melting away an unusually heavy snowpack, while a warm rain poured down for several days. Over a period of years, shrubs and small trees had grown up on the banks of the Methow River. When the floodwaters drastically raised the water level, uprooted brush formed temporary dams, which caused farmlands to be flooded and river banks to disintegrate. As the water sought to escape down the valley, it carved new channels through the land and near Pateros washed away an entire farm, dirt and all.

At Twisp, citizens worked day and night to contain the river. Big Perry Novotny, who weighed more than 300 pounds, was forced to sprint from the old red wooden bridge when it collapsed with him and two men on it. The newer concrete bridge was undermined and one end sagged. Whole houses from upstream Winthrop floated by. According to Mrs. Ben Nickell, a Twisp resident, the water was running so swiftly that it was higher in the middle than in the eddies.

Because the rising waters threatened to contaminate the town's water system, Charlie Schmidt, the town's tallest man, was elected to wade into the water to turn off the distribution pump. Unfortunately, Charlie couldn't swim a stroke, so he went in with a safety rope around him. He turned off the pump but lost his footing and had to be towed out.

The noise from the river was deafening because it rolled big boulders and gravel around as it rampaged along. For a week the river boiled down the valley, destroying or damaging every bridge from Mazama to Pateros. Twisp gave up the fight after two or three days and moved everything possible to high ground. The town was entirely isolated. A small aircraft which flew in and landed on the newly-seeded football field was the only communication with the outside world possible. When the flood subsided, the townspeople were able to repair the concrete bridge and get out of the valley to Brewster via the ancient wagon road. All available highway funds were summoned to repair the damage.

In 1953, a momentous meeting of highway boosters was held in the town of Okanogan, resulting in establishment of the North Cross-State Highway Association, later known as the North Cascades Highway Association. Representatives from Island, Whatcom, Skagit, Chelan, Okanogan, and Ferry counties voiced their ire over the fact that the southern 60 per cent of the State had five cross-mountain highways and the northern 40 per cent had none. A full-scale promotional campaign and plans to exert political pressure were discussed. Two annual meetings were scheduled, one on each side of the mountains. The presidency and vice presidency of the organization would alternate between the east and west. The first president was Sig Berglund of Sedro Woolley and the vice president, G. A. Ridpath of Okanogan.

Sig Berglund lost no time in getting started. He issued invitations to a meeting in Sedro Woolley to all legislators, senators, the governor, and other influential government officials. Without exception, every one of them replied "no," "previous commitment," or "can't come." On a Friday afternoon, thoroughly angered, Berglund sent each person a telegram cryptically stating, "Meeting cancelled due to lack of interest on the part of State officials." On Monday morning Berglund's phone rang incessantly; embarrassed officials wanted to know what was desired.

"We just don't want to be ignored," came the reply.

On the following Thursday, most of the invited officials appeared for a meeting, where the NCHA presented speakers in favor of renewing efforts to build a cross-mountain road. Elected officials could not ignore the pressure being exerted by the boosters, organized and numerous now. Many promised to support the effort, and the association agreed not to interfere with the details of the construction and routing but leave that to the state and federal road builders. It stated that members would exert all of their influence toward obtaining public support for appropriations.

The group mapped a campaign to gain support of the State Good Roads Association, which had a committee in each chamber of commerce. The theme for promotion of the road took a new direction at this point. For decades proponents had painted pictures of the need for a supply road between east and west; now the NCHA lauded the advantages of new recreational lands and the economic value of vast timber resources. By this time, freight travel was well established in a north-south direction on both sides of the mountains. Tourism was touted as a source of new jobs for the Methow and Skagit valleys, both chronically depressed. The NCHA planned a campaign covering a highway from Okanogan to the Olympic Peninsula, including a ferry from Whidbey Island to the Peninsula as a water highway.

The ebullience that marked the beginnings of the NCHA evaporated in December, 1954, when the State Highway Department presented a ten-year plan for highways at a Chamber of Commerce meeting in Bellingham that did *not* include the cross-mountain highway. Later that evening, as NCHA members dejectedly reviewed the bad news in a private conference with Bill Bugge, State Highway Director, Bugge suggested that the association approach the Bureau of Public Roads for appropriations because much of the North Cascades was now controlled by the federal government.

Meanwhile, the specter of factions working for other routes arose once more when Frank Haskell suggested to a group of port commissioners in Bellingham that a road might be put through the mountains on the old route surveyed decades before by the Great Northern. Headlines in the *Bellingham Herald* proclaimed, "Highway through Whatcom County!" Sig Hjaltalin, mayor of Bellingham and an NCHA member, met with Haskell in a private conference room to demand abandonment of discussion about a Mount Baker route. Hjaltalin's warning that a split in ranks would sabotage all the progress made was heeded and nothing more came of the Mount Baker concept.

Whether coincidental or because of the request of NCHA members, on February 24, 1955, U.S. Forest Ranger Frank Lewis of Marblemount told the Upper Skagit Booster Club (an ally of NCHA) that he had received a request for a huge timber sale in the Granite Creek area above Ross Dam. If such a sale were approved, Lewis commented, a road would have to be constructed from either the Methow Valley or Diablo, in order to remove the timber. The Granite Creek sale fell through, but in October, 1956, Al Frizzell of the United States Engineers started a survey for a bridge across the Skagit River and admitted the Mount Baker National Forest was considering a road to Thunder Basin to harvest timber. If built, the road would follow the proposed route of the North Cascades Highway.

During the 1955–56 meeting of the NCHA, presided over by President Jess Sapp, aging Otto Klement appeared to restate his support for the highway — which he had revived in 1919 through his editorial in the *Mount Vernon Argus*. Ray Jordan of the *Burlington Farm Journal* lent his pen to the cause by writing a series of colorful articles about the North Cascades.

In 1957, new governor Albert D. Rosellini, brought a renewed wave of optimism to highway supporters when he stated in his inaugural address that the North Cascades Highway was one of two new roads needed in the State. With this encouragement, Les Holloway, new NCHA president, met with the Bureau of Public Roads and the State and the two agreed to support the building of the segment from Diablo to Thunder.

State engineers Fred Walters and Walter Theiss were sent to explore the head of Thunder Creek as a possible continuation of the road. In order to get there, the two men entered the mountains via the Hart's Pass-Slate Creek road on horseback with a packer from Jack Wilson's ranch. At Ruby Creek the water ran so swiftly they could not proceed until they had constructed a footbridge by falling a tree across the stream. They proceeded on foot while the packer returned the horses to the Methow, trucking them around the mountains through Stevens Pass and up the Skagit Valley to Diablo. There Seattle City Light hauled horses, hay, and supplies to Thunder Arm, and Wilson and his helper, Bill Stokes, packed everything two more miles up Thunder Creek. In order to cross Thunder Creek the packers had to persuade the horses to go across an ancient, mossy, suspension bridge that undulated like a serpent. After five round trips to bring in supplies, the packers were thoroughly disgusted when the engineers only stayed one day in camp after a trip to Hoot Owl Pass, an almost vertical rampart at the head of the basin, convinced them that road building here was sheer folly.

Oddly, the man who had made the 1933 survey of the Early Winters area — Ike Munson — was transferred at this time as district engineer of the State Highway Department for the five counties of North Central Washington, including Okanogan. So to his office in September, 1957, fell the task of another survey to locate (a more detailed analysis than a survey) seven miles of road on the east side. At this time a pack trip of NCHA members and influential guests was organized and came over the mountains, with publicity designed to reach the public eye before the State convention in Longview of the Washington Good Roads Association.

For the horsemen — particularly the dudes — the trip could not be classified as fun. Faced with a deadline, the NCHA hastily put together the large band of horses required from several ranches. Strangers to each other, the horses squabbled and fought night and day. George Zahn's own horse bucked him off within full view of everyone, and the next day he reared and went over backwards with him — this time almost killing him. Zahn quipped that the worst thing about it was that he swallowed half his cigar and got sick. The yellowjackets were extremely active. One rider counted 190 lumps on his horse, a purebred Arabian that nearly died from the bites. Not knowing the techniques of the Forest Rangers, who galloped for several hundred yards whenever bees were encountered, the dudes halted and were attacked furiously by the yellowjackets. Horses bucked or ran away; cameras and other loose objects tied onto saddles flopped around and further frightened the horses. Several riders fell off. Fortunately, no one was hurt seriously, and Zahn later said that he spent most of that trip picking up people, glasses, cameras, and jackets. It's amazing that the journalists prepared glowing stories about the North Cascades.

The North Cascades Highway Association tried to stay in the limelight to build public support for the road. When Julia Butler Hansen, then head of the Roads and Bridges Committee, asserted that there was no public interest in such a highway, the association gathered together a caravan of ninety cars bearing 200 people from both sides of the mountains to prove her wrong. The stream of cars assembled at Playland Amusement Park north of Seattle and proceeded together to Olympia. Sig Berglund arranged with newspaper reporters and radio news commentators to bring roving transmitters to the rendezvous point and to interview caravanners. Representatives from KOMO-TV, radio station KJR, and others went along with the caravan, and the *Seattle P.I., Times* and local newspapers chimed in. Live news coverage was broadcast to the entire Northwest. When the caravanners reached the State Capitol in such force, legislators and senators had to listen. At the request of Paul McKay, district engineer, with the approval of Julia Butler Hansen (who was now convinced there *was* interest), Fred Martin sponsored a bill requesting an appropriation of $125,000 for surveying. Later $75,000 was set aside.

Now that the State was receptive to the North Cascades Highway, the association turned its attention to prodding the federal government. The Forest Service already had indicated interest in a road from Diablo to Thunder Basin to remove logs; in fact, logs taken out from the formation of Diablo Lake years before lay stacked high along Colonial Creek, awaiting some form of transport. Sig Hjaltalin and Fred Martin went to Portland to see the Forest Service, where Hjaltalin gave an eloquent plea about harvesting the timber:

> I have seen great cedar logs downed, some as much as six and eight feet in diameter lying down. It will just lay and rot and be a terrific fire hazard, a bug-breeding place. Who likes to look at a ragged stump, and logs so rotten one cannot even sit on it for a picnic. Truly we are the most wasteful people on earth.

An example of further waste because of no road was cited by John Pierce, who showed photographs of the drowned trees above Ross Dam. He also mentioned twenty-six patented mining claims within the North Cascades that could not be worked without roads.

In October, 1958, one million dollars was budgeted to build a highway from Diablo to Thunder Arm as a dual purpose road — for Forest Service use and as part of the future highway. The State followed by appropriating funds in January to improve the access roads from both the Skagit Valley and Methow Valley. Munson reported at this time that, if the road were built all at once, it could be done for eleven million. Instead, it was built piecemeal over the next fourteen years and cost twenty-three million dollars.

At first, Seattle City Light was cool toward the prospect of a highway, partly because Seattle support in general was lacking. Naturally that city was not eager to have traffic flowing over a North Cascades route instead of into Seattle from Snoqualmie Pass. Still, when mounting operating costs and lessening need forced abandonment of its railroad, City Light joined in urging the completion of the highway. At the mouth of Stevens Pass Highway, Wenatchee also bucked growing public opinion that a North Cascades Highway should be built without delay — except for its newspaper, the *World*, which steadfastly supported the highway.

Pressure on the state and federal agencies by the NCHA could not slacken, for annually a new crop of men had to be convinced of the wisdom of appropriations. The organization was original in its publicity schemes. In August, 1959, Charles Dwelley of the *Concrete Herald*, as newly elected president of the NCHA, adopted a slogan of "Across the Pass in Five Years," and entertained more than one hundred people at an ox-rib barbecue in Concrete.

When excessive rainfall in November sent mud and snowslides onto the Cascades, closing all four of the cross-mountain highways, the association, through Ralph Ferguson, mayor of Twisp, sent more than one hundred telegrams to Governor Rosellini saying, "We need another highway across the mountains."(However, it probably would have been closed, too.)

By February, 1960, a temporary bridge crossed the Skagit River at Diablo, after construction crews encountered such a swift flow of water that it bent the drilling derrick's A-frame. A crew was active also in the Early Winters Canyon at the east end of the route, doing preliminary work. Meanwhile, at the Legislative Interim Committee of Highways hearing in Wenatchee and a similar one in Mount Vernon, lobbyists from the NCHA presented pleas for further appropriations. Funds were made available to start work on the east end near Early Winters and to bring the old Skagit Gorge trail section between Newhalem and Diablo up to State standards.

On Labor Day of 1960, a publicity stunt was staged to show how even existing improvements had helped to speed travel across the mountains. Methow Valley residents challenged Skagit Valley citizens to a horseback race across the highway route. Horsemen drew lots. The Methow's contestant was a Forest Service employee, Jerry ("Dude") Sullivan, and the Skagit's was Oscar Peterson of Mount Vernon. Horses were to be stationed every eight or ten miles on the trail from Ruby Creek to Early Winters Resort, and riders were to change horses frequently. Since Peterson could not round up enough horses, he rode the entire distance with two purebred Arabians, alternately riding one and leading the other.

Dude Sullivan had nothing but trouble with the logistics of several horses and handlers. The horses were ordinary cow ponies, and some were slow. Bud Lloyd set out the day before the race with three of the horses via Hart's Pass Road, but had a flat tire and then got lost en route to Ruby Creek — so those three horses arrived too late to be stationed in position. Whitey Berg and Hank Dammann left at dawn from Early

Winters and went to their respective stations, but when Sullivan started out from Ruby Creek, he found that the first relief horse had broken loose and fled. The beginning horse went sixteen miles instead of eight. The day was rainy and the old Granite Creek Trail was full of mudholes, one 150 feet wide at Rainy Pass.

"It got so wet," said Sullivan, "that one stirrup stretched out a full inch longer than the other. This threw me off balance and gave me knee aches." Nevertheless, he made the fifty-three miles in eight hours, and Peterson was only an hour or so behind. At Early Winters Resort a hilarious group of highway boosters and newsmen had a huge party while awaiting the arrival of the contestants. Private bets inevitably developed with a pool for the one guessing the arrival time. As the winner, Sullivan received half of this sum, and also a souvenir saddlebag. Poor Oscar Peterson got nothing but the satisfaction that he had done the deed with only two horses.

19

Promotion on Horseback

When the summer sun shone in a blue sky, who could resist an invitation from highway boosters to go on a mountain pack trip. Members of the North Cascades Highway Association exerted more influence on legislators and journalists on horseback than in offices. Shepherding a long series of groups were the professional packers — men like lanky Jack Wilson, who was a Methow Valley businessman and president of the association in 1960–61. He had to assemble gentle horses accustomed to mountain trails, hire a top-notch cook, and attend to purchasing the myriads of small items that made the difference between pleasant living and misery. The packer was a combination guide, executive chef, first aid expert, activities director, historian, botanist, and mother hen. There were times in the mountains that required all the talents the packer had.

Previously employed as a construction worker on Grand Coulee Dam and the San Francisco Bay Bridge, Jack Wilson's first visit to the Methow Valley to look at property was inauspicious — a rattlesnake bit him. Fate intervened, perhaps, because during his visit to a Forest Ranger for treatment, Jack learned about the Early Winters Resort property, which was for sale. Wilson and his wife, Elsie, built several cabins and acquired about seventy-five head of horses and mules plus pack equipment. Elsie ran the resort and Jack went out on trips all season. His client list read like "Who's Who," including Justice William O. Douglas, governors Rosellini and

Evans, Allen Dulles, federal and state legislators, and other dignitaries — plus ordinary citizens and highway personnel. Groups usually consisted of twenty to thirty people.

Not all the trips were for highway boosters, of course; but many had publicity overtones for that purpose. Seldom were two trips alike; there are many variables in a mixture of people, weather and animals. During one publicity trip, Walt Straley, an executive from Seattle, was out hunting with Wilson, when Wilson tried to flush a deer in the thicket above. A rock the size of a boxcar broke loose and plunged down the mountainside, narrowly missing Straley, then split into several pieces as large as an automobile. The huge pieces mainlined down the slope and swept onto a meadow below with such force that some boulders rolled a quarter mile before stopping. Later that week, while Jack and a couple of men were fishing in a lake near Chuchuwateen Creek, a lightning strike set fire to the brush and they had to put it out. One man's horse quit the scene at full gallop, going a half mile before it skidded to a halt, turned around and returned to its master.

It seemed that everything happened during a hunting trip scheduled one fall for Governor Rosellini and friends. On the scheduled morning of departure, all were present except the governor; he was delayed in Olympia because an elderly woman protesting some matter insisted on eating breakfast on the porch of the governor's mansion. The guests went on ahead with the assistant packers and Jack waited for Rosellini. When he finally arrived, the two men went by truck twenty miles over a rough mountain road, then mounted horses for another twenty-two miles of high mountain trails — part of it in darkness. Along a section of trail near Rock Creek, part of the Cascade Crest Trail, the path narrowed to about thirty-six inches above a 1500-foot cliff. Wilson went ahead on his horse leading the pack mule and waited for the governor to come through. Rosellini, fearful of heights, had opted to walk.

While he waited, Jack let the two animals graze for a minute. Tied to the horse's saddle by a rope, the mule browsed placidly until the horse stepped over the rope where it drooped on the ground. When the mule lifted its head, the saddle horse went crazy with fright because the rope came up between his hind legs. Still tied to the mule, he bucked so furiously that Wilson's rifle was flung out of the scabbard and items came out of his pack. While this exhibition was going on, Rosellini came around the final bend of the cliff trail in time to be knocked down by the frantic horse. Jack finally managed to get out his knife and sever the rope between the animals to put an end to the fracas.

After dark, the two men got to a point called the Devil's Stairway at 7,600-foot elevation, where there was one switchback above a sheer 1,000-foot cliff. Jack said later that he didn't dare let the governor get off and walk along the precipice in darkness.

"I just told him to keep the reins even and snug and let his horse follow mine. He did just fine and we got to Hopkins Pass OK and caught up with our party."

The governor was able to stay for only two days, then rode out with Wilson over the same steep trail.

Wilson's camps could not be called spartan. He had a fourteen-by-sixteen-foot tent for cooking, another the same size for dining, and four or five others for sleeping, plus a dozen two-man tents. These were left in place between trips so that all Wilson had to pack in was the current food. Under the old law of the range, transient hikers were welcome to use the equipment and a sign proclaimed "Use the camp if you like. Leave it as you found it." Most people heeded this. After a party arrived at camp, horses and mules were turned loose to graze, with bells placed on key animals. Being a clannish lot, the stock grazed quietly and such dispersal prevented damage to any one spot. When Wilson had a large party like those from the Wilderness Society or the American Forestry Association, he made camp at a central point, then sent his assistants out with small groups. This method avoided the feeling of mass handling.

On one such trip Mrs. Marx of the Marx Toy Company expressed a desire to see a good lightning storm. She got her wish. About twelve people went to Three Fools Peak, about 8,300-foot elevation, tied their horses when they could go no farther on them, and walked to the top for a picnic. Suddenly there was an ugly ring of clouds around Jack Mountain, "like the clouds were going to pick the mountain out of the earth," Wilson said later. Lightning was flashing everywhere in the clouds, and the storm moved toward the party. Wilson got the group quickly down the mountain to the horses; they mounted and rode about two miles to the Cascade Crest Trail, but were unable to outrun the storm. Hailstones up to five-eighths of an inch hit them. The worst thing to do in such a situation was to tie to a tree or even get near one, rather, the party spread out so that, if one got hit, not all would be stricken. There was a powerful smell of ozone, and hailstones jumped four feet in the air.

"We were inside the lightning storm, and when this occurs," said Wilson, "you hardly see it at all — just little flickers of light all around you — but, boy, the noise!"

Suddenly a young mule panicked and went galloping by the whole string, not on the trail but through the brush twenty feet below and across a rockslide. Its rider was screaming and hanging on. Wilson managed to get down to drag her off the mule unhurt. Within minutes the storm had passed, and Jack asked Mrs. Marx how she liked getting her wish. All she could say was, "Wow!"

Unpredictable weather in the North Cascades brought snow during every month of the year; campers sometimes awoke with as much as eighteen inches of snow on top of them. It never lasted long, and it wasn't the depth that was critical, but the tendency of the snow to blow into drifts across narrow trails. Under these circumstances, hapless pack trip guests simply had to wait until the snow melted.

Jack Wilson had the pleasure of packing for Justice William O. Douglas, well-known as an experienced mountain man. After arrangements were made by telephone, Wilson met Douglas at Intercity Airport near Twisp, and "got the dog-gonedest looking over you ever saw from those piercing blue eyes. There wasn't a doubt in my mind that, if he hadn't liked something he saw, he would have gotten right back in his plane and taken off again."

In his active outdoor life Douglas had been rolled on by a

horse, breaking twenty-seven ribs, which had grown back together in such a way that he sometimes found it difficult to
breathe — indeed, he had relearned breathing in a new way.
But he was a tough, knowledgeable man; in fact, he was preparing a story about the North Cascades when he packed in
with Wilson. Douglas was keenly interested in the later proposal to make the North Cascades National Park a reality.

The pack trips were not only pleasure trips, but reconnaissance by key officials in the Highway Department and governmental offices. All of the variations of the route were
explored in person, before decisions were made. Members of
the North Cascades Highway Association made such trips at
their own expense, dedicated solely to completion of the
long-awaited highway.

20

Construction and Contention

While promoters turned their attention to the North Cascades Highway, Cascade Pass — abandoned as a road route — was selected for intensive study of glaciers in 1957 because of its isolation. A United States Geological Survey crew under the direction of Mark F. Meier installed basic living quarters and scientific equipment near the South Cascade Glacier, about eight miles from the end of the Stehekin Road. Everything was built to withstand snow loads up to twenty-five feet deep and winds up to 150 miles per hour. The survey team measured total winter snow and water discharged into South Cascade Lake from the glacier, and from the glacial lake into the Cascade River. Results of the investigation showed that the lake had grown from two to fifty acres over a twenty-year period. Carbon testing of a totally preserved stump recovered from the ice showed it to be 300 years old; and the team found that the glacier moved about seventy feet per year — a very swiftly moving body of ice.

Working from a base at Slate Creek, another Geological Survey team worked at mapping wilderness that had never before been explored. Known as the Slate Pass Project, the work was carried out by a team of twelve men and helicopters furnished by Whirl-Wide Helicopters of Fresno, California.

When the Forest Service announced its intention of building a road from Diablo to Thunder Basin to remove logs, the Sierra Club went on record opposing further logging. The *Sierra Club Bulletin* stated that, although logging might be necessary on ninety per cent of the forest land, preservation programs for at least ten per cent should be emphasized. It criticized the Forest Service, saying:

> When the forest service, in planning activities such as these three [Thunder and two in California] makes it clear that it does not intend to expand its wilderness dedications to meet the needs of today and the future, it becomes obvious why, when so many conservationists have decided to get the wilderness preservation job done, they just turn to another agency, the National Park Service.

The North Cascades Highway Association, on the other hand, had already gone on record in protest of the locking up of forest lands, particularly the 801,000-acre North Cascades Primitive Area. Now the Glacier Peak Wilderness Area was being considered and, despite unified resistance to the concept by each of the counties involved — Whatcom, Skagit, Okanogan, and Chelan — on September 15, 1960, Glacier Peak Wilderness was created by Ezra T. Benson, Secretary of Agriculture. It was an immense area taking in Glacier Peak, Hurricane Peak, Mount Cheval, and thirty other major peaks and valleys in between.

In 1961, the Wagner Mill at Twisp laid off an entire shift of men because it could not get enough logs to supply its mill full-time. The closure was only one of the economic woes of Okanogan County towns, and Okanogan County was declared officially a distressed area. The Twisp Chamber of Commerce appealed to the federal government, and together with Jack Abrams and the Okanogan County Commission, suggested that the North Cascades Highway be built with Federal Distressed Area funds, because completion would help alleviate unemployment there.

That same year, there was a vacancy in the State Highway Commission and Okanogan County highway boosters aggressively campaigned for the appointment of Republican George Zahn. It was a measure of Zahn's stature that not only were Republicans campaigning for him, but so were members of the Democratic Party — Leonard Therriault, State Democratic Committeeman; George Wilson, Okanogan County Democratic Chairman; State Representative John

Goldmark; and Senator Hallower from Okanogan, who found himself plugging for his former opponent in the race for state senator. Governor Rosellini appointed Zahn.

An ardent supporter of the North Cascades Highway, Zahn was in a position to influence legislators favorably for appropriations; and members of the association credited him with "getting the ball rolling."

Governor Rosellini came to the June, 1962, NCHA meeting to indicate his support of the highway effort; and the list of other dignitaries who now endorsed the highway by attending that meeting was impressive. That same year Bill Bugge, State highway director, verified that financing of the highway seemed assured, with the west side receiving funds from the Federal Bureau of Public Roads, the east from the State of Washington.

Meantime, on the east side, Mac Lloyd of Twisp, as subcontractor for Goodfellow Brothers, Wenatchee, was working on the initial clearing of roadway and building of temporary bridges from the Methow Valley toward Washington Pass. At first it was a logging operation, with timber being cut and stacked until a rough road could be built and trucks brought in to remove the logs. Working ahead of the clearing contractor were the survey and location crews of the State. Jack Wilson installed and moved their camps whenever needed.

The first camp was near Indian Creek about six miles above the mouth of Early Winters Creek, the second at Willow Creek, then Cutthroat, and so on. Between Lone Fir and Cutthroat, rattlesnakes were a constant menace; it was common to encounter several a day. Until bulldozers built a rough roadway, access to the surveyors' camps was by horseback and the combination of horses and machinery was sometimes hazardous. Al Gracey, resident engineer, suffered two broken ribs when his horse became frightened by a dozer and bucked him off. Removed to the hospital for taping up, Gracey was back within a short time, to be greeted at the camp by a sign in the shape of a grinning horse's head which read: "Gracey's Point. Let's kiss and make up." His men denied any responsibility for the kidding.

Survey crews enjoyed the best of food as some compensation for their rough life and isolation. One of the best and most versatile cooks was Tom ("Sonny") Martin, who was not only a cook but also a demolition expert and hard rock miner. In addition, he made furniture for the camp with a chain saw. Vandalism by bears was always a problem, and whenever the entire crew was away, a camp watcher was hired to scare them off. At Cutthroat Camp, when the returning crew puzzled over finding bullet holes in the tent, the furniture, and even the kitchen stove, the camp watcher told a fantastic story about being attacked by wild turkeys and elephants. Investigation of the garbage dump revealed dozens of empty liquor bottles to be the cause of the imaginary fray.

There was little entertainment for the men on either survey or construction crews. Watching deer became commonplace, while swimming in the glacier-fed creeks was only for the hardy. Inevitably the crews enlivened their daily lives with rough humor. There was a flamboyant roller operator named Cleo who was always wrecking his cars. He drove a heavy auto so recklessly that he often banged the oil pan from the bottom of it, letting all the oil run out; his fenders were dented and headlights and taillights were off. Instead of driving more cautiously, he welded a skid plate on the bottom of the car. One night his buddies painted the car's fenders orange and affixed orange flags to all four corners, "so he could tell where they were." Before long, Cleo had wrecked that car beyond repair, and while driving his wife's new car to work, he misjudged a corner again and sent it over a cliff into Cooper Basin.

A few men brought their families to live in the woods in tents. At Lone Fir Campground, under the shadow of Silver Star Mountain, three families roughed it. The men worked as much as six days straight, but the wives were accustomed to amusing themselves. Mrs. Robert Adler had spent all but six months of her married life in a construction trailer and had a three-year-old to watch. Violet Rickell mothered the wild animals — a deer that licked a salt block ten feet from her kitchen stove, "Lonesome George," a magpie that came in for daily handouts, a couple of snowshoe rabbits, and dozens of small birds and chipmunks that enjoyed scraps from the kitchen. Ella Hoefs was a rockhound and spent her spare time with a pick, once finding a rare tourmaline.

Running out of ice was a problem, because it provided the only refrigeration; for baths, if one wasn't brave enough to jump in the chilly creek, there was a galvanized tub.

Workers Gene Dodd and Al Person pitched a tent just below Liberty Bell Mountain and lived there all summer, taking snow out of an all-summer snowslide below the mountain for refrigeration. Dodd's family came to visit occasionally, and his three boys were especially intrigued by the fact that garter snakes slept under their cots, and curious bears poked in and out of camp constantly.

One veteran construction worker, C. Y. ("Cally") Hotchkiss, had come over the highway route in 1900 with his homesteader parents, horses, and cattle, walking across Cascade Pass and down through Rainy Pass.

From Cutthroat Creek to Rainy Pass the construction crew fought their way through solid rock. Though forced to use dynamite, they modified the charge; if they had used a full charge, it would have flattened trees on both sides of the road. Scenic preservation was a prime factor in the construction contract. All of the rubble was hauled out or transported to a different location as fill, not dumped into unsightly heaps or into the streams.

The North Cascades Highway was indeed unique because its planning committee included a landscape architect. Previously, roads were often carved straight through the land, leaving terrible scars, while tall trees on either side prevented motorists from enjoying any nearby scenery. Judicious cutting of a few trees here and there beside the North Cascades Highway made it possible for a traveler to see the mountain peaks. Replanting of grass on gently sloping banks adjacent to the roads lessened the impact of the asphalt ribbon on the land, while deer found the new pastures of planted grass delectable. To avoid scarring of the area along Ross Lake and Ruby Creek, Harold Chriswell of the Forest Service put up a battle to utilize a tunnel from Thunder Arm through the mountain, lobbying so tenaciously that planners began to refer to it as "Chriswell's damned tunnel." Although the idea was defeated, the highway builders compromised by routing the road over the mountains above Ross Lake, instead of skirting along the canyon by Ruby.

By spring of 1962 the ticklish job of widening the old Gorge trail from Newhalem to Diablo was given to Canadian firms: Highway Construction, Ltd. and Emil Anderson Construction Company of Richmond, B.C. The Skagit Gorge was still claiming victims. In late October, Jack Turner of Clear Lake was buried by fifty tons of rock while he operated his shovel; and only a week later Glenn Stafford of Concrete was buried in the cab of his tractor. The mountain had sent down one warning boulder, which bounded in front of Stafford, but before he could back out of the area, the slide engulfed him. Thereafter this section of road was declared to be so dangerous that the school bus from Diablo to Concrete drove empty along the canyon road, while the school children, wearing hard hats like construction workers, tiptoed through on foot; it was feared that the vibration from the big bus might set off slides.

While machinery was working in the Gorge, a lookout was posted where he could see the entire mountainside above. If any part of it started to move, he sounded an alarm. Even so, Alfred Clark of Marblemount was lost in April, 1963, while scaling rock, although 20,000 cubic yards of loose rubble had been blasted off only two days prior to the accident.

In 1963, the North Cascades Highway Association adopted the slogan, "Thirty Miles to Go." By then, only the segment between Ross Lake and Rainy Pass was raw land.

Meanwhile, the preservationists, through the North Cascades Conservation Council of Seattle and Congressman Tom Pelly, pressed for the establishment of a vast North Cascades National Park. Pelly requested a moratorium on further logging of the area adjacent to the North Cascades Highway. Many highway supporters feared that such a move might totally halt construction, if adopted. Congressman Jack Westland countered by pointing to the huge areas already set aside in Glacier Peak Wilderness Area, North Cascades Primitive Area, and others, indicating that the shortage of logs already was acute. Secretary of the Interior Stewart

Udall and Agriculture Secretary Orville Freeman authorized a North Cascades Study Team to investigate the best use of the lands between Mount Rainier, south of Seattle, and the Canadian border. Senator Henry Jackson, trying to walk a tightrope between preservationists and park promoters, lumbermen and highway boosters, gave a resumé of the status of the North Cascades Highway on May 15, 1964, indicating that the construction crews would be separated by only thirty miles by fall.

As if there weren't enough rainfall in the North Cascades, scientists in April, 1964, inexplicably conducted a six-month cloud-seeding experiment to increase the runoff into the Skagit River by fifteen per cent. Stuart Shumway, weather modification supervisor for the Conservation Department, used ground-based generators that sprayed silver iodide solution into passing storm clouds, causing water vapor to collect and fall as rain. Farmers in the Skagit Valley raised a big storm of their own, claiming that the additional rains were ruining their crops, and in January, 1965, presented a petition against cloud-seeding signed by 600 residents. Unusually heavy snows that winter amplified the feeling of many that there should be no "monkeying around with the natural weather." In the always treacherous Skagit Gorge, seven big slides came down in early January, bringing snow up to twelve feet deep and slides as long as 150 feet. The road became totally impassable, and Diablo residents were cut off from all outside access except by helicopter. Some who had left for the holiday season were unable to return home.

The severe winter weather continued on into spring, and repeatedly slides plagued the Baker Lake powerhouse near Concrete. Trees, mud and rock slid down near the workings, and on May 18 a gigantic earth slide completely destroyed the powerhouse. It had rained all weekend, and about three A.M., watchers were alerted by a moving wall of mud that came from the canyon south of the structure. It moved in and piled up high against the building, making it groan ominously. All personnel inside were evacuated. Shutting off the power plant before they left, the last of the men departed by boat as the hill above the powerhouse began to disintegrate.

Rolling and sliding, the mud, rock, and trees pushed against the building until the sheer weight broke through the top story. The roof collapsed onto the first floor with a violent roar, sending a cloud of dust high into the sodden sky. Still the rains came and all day further mudslides mixed with rock advanced across the building, twisting girders and crumbling the concrete supports. The penstock on the new generator broke, releasing water stored in the tunnel and in the surge tank, and the tank was crushed. The huge generator installed in 1960, with a rotor weighing over 200 tons, lay under the rubble.

Damage was estimated at more than five million dollars. While the upper Baker powerhouse struggled to keep up with power demands, Morrison-Knudson started clean up and repairs. By late August, three months later, the big generators still had not been located under the mud.

In December, 1964, the State Highway Commission allocated more than one million dollars of Bureau of Public Roads funds for construction on the west side. Senators Warren Magnuson and Henry Jackson, and Representatives Tom Foley and Lloyd Meeds teamed up to make a united request for funds from the Federal Public Lands Act, securing an additional half million, an unprecedented grant because the fund usually conferred money only once to a given area.

The west side construction was particularly difficult. Construction people first worked along the treacherous Skagit Gorge and over the mountain above Ross, then, as rough roadway was built eastward, maneuvered trucks around Horsetail Falls, later renamed John Pierce Falls. This waterfall fell in two sections with a narrow ledge interrupting it, across which had to move the heavy equipment. The ledge even tilted downhill slightly. Chuck Wolf was the foreman for a Goodfellow crew and supervised the preparation of the ledge to accommodate the vehicles, sanding and graveling part of it; yet the roadbed remained narrow and dangerous. During the initial clearing in 1965, a big tractor working there went over the ledge into the canyon hundreds of feet below when its brakes failed, but the operator jumped to safety. When Wolf brought in big off-highway trucks to use in the clearing operation east of Horsetail, the drivers looked at the ledge and declared they just didn't want to go through. As he was responsible for the job, Wolf finally offered to drive the first truck across the ledge. With knees shaking so badly that he thought the drivers would notice, he climbed into a truck and drove about ten feet. The driver of the truck Wolf had commandeered, stung by the silent rebuke, wrenched the door open and roared at Wolf that if he could drive across, the regular drivers could.

No trucks were lost, but besides the narrowness of the ledge, which left one of the dual wheels on the outside edge of the truck hanging over into space, there was the problem of icicles which formed every morning. Workers had to get across before they formed. Each evening Wolf sent a tractor over the ledge before the trucks to knock down the icicles. These spectacular spires, which hung from the cliffs adjacent to the falls, built up swiftly to as much as two or three tons.

The men worked with unstable ground during the clearing. One morning Wolf's crew arrived at the work site, two miles east of Horsetail at No-name Creek, to find that only a bit of exhaust pipe from a bulldozer marked the spot where their equipment was buried.

Despite the hazards and setbacks encountered, the construction crews steadily worked from both ends of the road to close the gap that divided east from west — only about 20 miles by December, 1965.

21

East and West Are Joined

Just as everything seemed to be moving ahead smoothly, both in the political arena and the mountains, the North Cascades Study Team released its recommendations in Seattle on January 6, 1966. Among its proposals were the setting aside of vast new areas of wilderness and a North Cascades National Park. Commercial use of the North Cascades Highway was frowned upon, and in the ensuing discussions some outdoor enthusiasts proposed that the entire highway construction project be halted. However, few took such an extreme stand, and a corridor was provided in the master plan for the road. The thrust remained for the road to be a scenic highway, not an access for logging, mining, or development.

In July, highway funds were bolstered by $400,000 of federal funds from a seven-million-dollar "make-work" fund that was propping up the economy at the time. The windfall was matched by State money, and construction moved ahead rapidly.

In 1964, a new governor, Dan Evans, had taken the helm of Washington government. An ardent outdoorsman, Evans had hiked, skiied, flown over, and ridden through the North Cascades country. While he was anxious to protect the mountains from exploitation, he also recognized the need for a cross-mountain road and forest management that provided jobs for Washington citizens. In order to see the highway progress firsthand, Governor Dan took a horseback trip in late August of 1966, from Silver Star camp to Ross Lake with his five-year-old son, Danny. Little Danny was mounted on an old gray mare and, despite his youth, was a good traveler — even on the old Granite Creek trail with its deep bogs and wet trees.

At Ross Lake, Harold Chriswell of the Forest Service arranged for a helicopter tour to parts of the North Cascades that few have ever seen. At one point, when the copter sat down near a lookout station, the young attendant proved to be a youth who had been a member of Evans's Boy Scout troop. Back at Ross Lake again, the governor and his party went on board a Seattle City Light tug for a tour of the lake, followed by a barbecue at Sedro Woolley.

A month later Evans was back for the annual meeting of the NCHA in Washington Pass. Dressed informally, the youthful governor spoke before a podium made from a stump, which rested on a flatbed truck. To the surprised pleasure of the assembly of 800 or 900 supporters, he announced that he hoped to double the amount of State money available annually for completion of the road. While Evans's two young sons watched, he and Don Manning, planning and research engineer for the Bureau of Public Roads, jointly ran a noisy jackhammer to dramatize the cooperation of state and federal governments. They had intended to set off a spectacular dynamite charge, but fire danger was too high.

K. K. Larsen Construction Company of Seattle in 1968 gained the contract to build Horsetail Falls Bridge, which required a 335-foot steel span. Workmen swinging in boatswain's chairs from the cliffs above the falls drilled through rock to provide anchoring for the piers with great steel anchors. Because the canyon is about 200 feet deep, there was no way to get to the bottom of the chasm to pour concrete piers, so a high cable was rigged across the canyon, from which all materials — including wet concrete — were suspended and lowered into place below. A heavy crane at one end of the cable handled placement of the materials. Before the girders were installed, a net was stretched across the canyon under the planned span to catch any falling workman. During the job the steel fabricator who supplied the girders was closed down by Internal Revenue Service officials, who impounded completed girders at the factory. Larsen appealed successfully for release of the girders, but there was a delay which extended into 1969.

Each bridge girder was about 110 feet in a single piece, ten feet deep, and weighed eighteen tons. The massive pieces were hauled one at a time up the narrow road from Newhalem, barely making it along the one-way stretch by the old gorge tunnel. The road had to be reinforced up to Horsetail Falls to support the weight; and once the truck arrived, there was little working space left to unload it. By first attaching one end of the girder to the traveling crane on the high cable, men were able to ease the girder slowly off the truck. The crane hung out over the canyon at its maximum reach; calculations of load and balance had to be exact to avoid sending crane and girder into the canyon below. All went smoothly; once the girders were across, completion came speedily.

In accordance with environmental standards adhered to in the construction, Larsen darkened the concrete to match nearby rocks; even the newly blasted rock faces were darkened to minimize the scarring. Historic spawning creeks like Ruby were safeguarded. Both residents and Forest Service personnel urged that money be provided to build recreational sites at logical points along the way.

In September, 1968, a crude pioneer road finally existed between the east and west segments of the highway; and a jubilant celebration was held at Rainy Pass. Four-wheel drive vehicles, dune buggies, cycles, and horses met for official joining ceremonies. To be a part of the historic first crossing, 400 or 500 vehicles lined up at Thunder Arm about daybreak on September 29. A holiday mood prevailed, even though the air was chilly as the motley caravan started east. Most of the road was adequate, but beyond Ross Dam the narrow trail still clung to the mountainside precariously and some small streams were still unbridged. The caravan made it to Rainy Pass in about two and a half hours; when it came into view, a big welcoming cheer went up from the eastsiders, who had been able to come on finished road most of the way. As the two groups slowly approached each other, Les Holloway of

Twisp mounted the hood of one jeep, John Pierce of Bellingham another, and the two vehicles came together — bumper
to bumper — so the two pioneers could clasp hands in a
symbolic joining of the two sides of the mountains. The
crowd of about 2,000 applauded wildly.

It was a politician's field day; everyone who could claim
some part in the planning or funding of the highway came.
Senator Warren Magnuson dropped in by helicopter; Representatives Tom Foley and Lloyd Meeds, the State senators,
and mayors of all nearby cities and towns appeared. Ken King,
current president of the NCHA, introduced Governor Dan
Evans. Eyes glowing with satisfaction, Evans lauded the ac-
complishments and added that, if he were reelected in
November, he would get the road completed for travel by the
end of his term. Charles Prahl, director of highways, added
his comments. In a carnival atmosphere on the warm fall day,
the crowd devoured chili and hamburgers provided by the
Winthrop Kiwanis Club.

Three days later, President Lyndon B. Johnson signed the
North Cascades National Park bill into law; with its passage,
the Forest Service lost jurisdiction over 301,000 acres to the
National Park and 107,000 to the Recreational Areas in the
Skagit District alone. Although the majority of the local
county residents had worked against the park, they set out
realistically to cooperate with the new staffs. By October 16, a
Skagit County Advisory Board was established as a liaison
with the park administration. Its chairman, David McIntyre,
Jr., commented, "The North Cascades Park is here. . . . For
those of us who might have questioned the idea in the beginning, it behooves us to work now for its full development."

Privately owned Puget Power & Light Company labored to
complete recreational facilities on Baker Lake and Lake
Shannon, to accommodate visitors from the highway. It constructed viewpoints, access roads, parking for fishermen, and
planted a million fingerling trout in Baker Lake in 1968 and
1969. The Cascade Northern Construction Company completed a two-year project of clearing floating logs from Lake
Shannon, to make its waters safe for small boats.

Awakening to the potential impact of the hordes of visitors

on its valleys, both the Skagit and Methow finally engaged in facelifting of business establishments. The ancient inn at Marblemount, Log Cabin Inn, was remodeled, yet retained its original narrow rooms from miners' days. At Winthrop, Mrs. Kathryn Wagner, civic-minded widow of lumberman Otto Wagner, offered to help the town in an effort to remodel itself into an old-time western community. With the help of the Kiwanis Club, the project proceeded at a hectic pace. Bob Jorgenson, an artist-architect, masterminded the redesigning of the new-old town. Twenty-two stores developed false store fronts. Raised wooden sidewalks were built and covered with shingled roofs. The old Winthrop Cafe became Sam's Place, with a false front that made it look like a livery stable. At its corner location, H & J Hardware built a cupola complete with an old bell obtained from Entiat, Washington. As in the saloons of yesteryear, a huge figure of a reclining woman was painted on the wall of Three-Fingered Jack's Tavern. On one building, artist Chet Endrizzi painted a reproduction of the famous Bull Durham Tobacco sign — a snorting bull.

While the townspeople made their last-minute preparations for traffic, the construction crews were putting the finishing touches on the highway and completing the bridges. At Concrete the new Baker River Bridge was rising, a 563-foot bridge built by Sea and Shore Piledriving of Seattle. In the summer of 1971, six giant girders came through the Skagit Valley for Panther Creek Bridge beyond Horsetail Falls, each weighing 98,000 pounds and 130 feet long — so long that on a detour road bypassing Lillian Creek the Rucker Brothers trucks were mere inches from dropping off a 700-foot embankment, while the ends of the girders brushed the inside cliff of a previous curve in the road.

On the east side, James Parkhill was the project engineer for the State Highway Department, working on the North Cascades Highway between 1968 and 1973. Construction camps were set up all along the route — four big trailers near Mazama for maintenance crews, a camp at Indian Creek near Pilchuck, others at Lone Star, Cutthroat Creek, Famine Creek, and Whistler Peak. During the winter of 1971–72, an avalanche wiped out the Whistler cabin, destroying everything. Weather always was the construction man's worst enemy in the North Cascades, so variable that on a July day in 1968, it was eighty degrees all day and fifteen degrees by the next morning with a foot and a half of snow on the ground.

During the summer and fall of 1971, a crew from C. V. Wilder Company roughed in the roadbed, shaped it, put in crushed rock preparatory to paving, and left for the winter. The following March, Chuck Wolf, who now worked for Wilder, and Tom Simpson of the Bureau of Public Roads went from Thunder Arm in a snowmobile to see what condition the road was in. About three miles west of Granite Creek they came upon a huge slide, which had come across Granite Creek and jammed up the water so that a big lake had formed. Only a small run-off stream rumbled through the debris. The slide was about fifty feet deep in the roadbed; and the two dismayed men concluded that there was about 250,000 yards of material to remove — a big setback if their work was to be completed by the September, 1972, opening deadline.

Twenty men and a crew of big Euclid trucks were ordered in just to remove the slide. The first problem was to get a tractor to the top of the slide, so that the material could be whittled down. After three tries, an operator made it. It was impossible to be sure that further slides would not be triggered by removal of the debris. Water continued to run through the material from the dammed creek. One "catskinner" rode a small slide from top to bottom of the original slide, unhurt. Two operators quit, too apprehensive of the situation. The crew removed rock and dirt from the lower side of the dam, thinning out the barrier as much as possible, until it was only ten to fifteen feet thick. Then a bold bulldozer operator made a decisive, speedy pass at the remainder, sweeping halfway across and backing out swiftly. The water boiled through the opening and battered down the remaining debris. Because it was a spawning stream, the crew carefully reconstructed the bed, spacing out some rocks for fish havens, removing others. Their remodeling job won them a letter of commendation from the Fish and Game Department.

Pressure for completion was extreme during the last few months, as extensive publicity had already been given out on the September opening. Wilder Company praised the friendly cooperation between all of the agencies and contractors working on the road that summer.

"We worked like brothers," said Wolf, "trading off equipment and men when needed. We made official charges on our books but, you know, when we were all done, the charges were so even that we called it 'no charge' between us all."

Under the pressure and long hours, the men on the surfacing crew were about to crack up by midsummer. One big, tough, equipment operator sat in Wolf's office and cried like a child out of sheer fatigue and frustration. To relieve the tension the company threw a weekend party, inviting wives and girl friends for a Saturday night fish fry. The change of pace worked wonders for all except Ben Day, a well-liked teamster who dropped dead on the dance floor of a heart attack about midnight.

Wilder's paving crews, hampered by the untimely loss of a crane over a cliff, worked up to the morning of the September 2 opening date. Figuratively, at least, the asphalt was still smoking when the caravan of cars streamed over the highway on that day.

Northern Washington was in two parts no longer; it was joined by the North Cascades Highway, an effort started in 1814 — 158 years since Alexander Ross first searched for a trail from Fort Okanogan to Puget Sound.

The impact of the completed highway in 1972 upon northern Washington was quite different from that contemplated originally. The road no longer was to fill the needs of miners, ranchers, and lumbermen because, by the time it was finished, most of the North Cascades had been placed in some form of protected recreational status. Instead, the highway primarily provided access to a vast playground and afforded economic opportunities to the residents of foothill valleys in furnishing amenities to tourists.

Designed in a period of keen interest in environmental protection, the North Cascades Highway lies gently upon the land without severe scarring of its surroundings. It has made a gift of vision to the motorist — the opportunity for Americans to see their own Alps, the North Cascades Mountains. The highway had taken a century and a half to build. It was the last major highway in the United States to be built through previously untouched lands. The North Cascadians had their road.

Bibliography

BOOKS AND PAMPHLETS

Abrams, Ernest R. *Power in Transition*. New York: Charles Scribner's Sons, 1940.

Andrews, Ralph W. *This Was Logging*. Seattle: Superior Publishers, 1964.

Bancroft, Hubert Howe. *History of Washington, Idaho and Montana*. San Francisco: The History Company, 1890.

Bulletin No. 84, Railway and Locomotive Historical Society, Boston, 1951.

Case, Robert O., and Case, Victoria. *Last Mountains*. Portland: Metropolitan Press, 1945.

Cooley, Leland S. *God's High Table*. Garden City: Doubleday & Company, 1962.

Cornwall, Bruce. *Life Sketch of Pierre Barlow Cornwall*. San Francisco: Stanley-Taylor Company, 1906.

Dow, Edson. *Adventure in the Northwest*. Wenatchee: Outdoor Publishing Company, 1964.

Dryden, Cecil. *Up the Columbia for Furs*. Caldwell: Caxton Printers, 1950.

Edson, Lelah Jackson. *The Fourth Corner*. Seattle: Craftsman Press, 1968.

Fries, U. E. *From Copenhagen to Okanogan*. Caldwell: Caxton Printers, 1949.

Hazard, Joseph T. *Snow Sentinels of the Pacific Northwest*. Seattle: Lowman & Hanford Co., 1932.

Holbrook, Stewart H. *Far Corner*. New York: The MacMillan Company, 1952.

197

————. *Illustrated History of Skagit and Snohomish Counties*. Interstate Publishing Company, 1906.

Jeffcott, P. W. *Chechaco and Sourdough*. Bellingham: Pioneer Printing Company, 1963.

Kerr, Harry J. *History of the Town of Okanogan and The First National Bank*. Okanogan: Independent Press, 1931.

Kramer, Arthur. *History of the Puget Sound Power & Light Company*. Seattle: The PSP & L Company, 1939.

Lavender, David. *Land of Giants*. Garden City: Doubleday & Company, 1958.

Lee, W. Storrs. *Washington State*. New York: Funk & Wagnalls, 1969.

McKee, Bates. *Cascadia*. New York: McGraw-Hill Book Company, 1972.

McWilliams, Mary. *Seattle Water Department History*. Seattle: City of Seattle, 1955.

Peattie, Roderick, ed. *The Cascades, Mountains of the Pacific Northwest*. Seattle: Lowman & Hanford Co., 1932.

Quinby, E. J. *Short Circuit Bulletin*, Texas Division, Electric Railroaders' Association, Inc., December, 1965.

Rahm, David A. and Easterbrook, Don. *Landforms of Washington; The Geologic Environment*. Bellingham: Union Printing Company, 1970.

Ray, Verne F. *The Sanpoil and Nespelem*. Seattle: University of Washington Press, 1933.

Ross, James Delmage. *City Light, The Municipal Light and Power System of Seattle, Washington*. Chicago: The Public Ownership League of America, 1928.

Roth, Lottie R. *History of Whatcom County*. Seattle: Pioneer Historical Publishing Company, 1926.

Ruby, Robert H. and Brown, John A. *Half-Sun on the Columbia*. Norman: University of Oklahoma Press, 1965.

Rusk, C. E. *Tales of a Western Mountaineer*. Boston: Houghton Mifflin Company, 1924.

Smith, Marian W., ed. *Indians of the Urban Northwest*. New York: Columbia University Press, 1949.

Steele, Richard and others. *History of North Central Washington*. Seattle: Western Historical Publishing Company, 1904.

Wight, E. L.; Mitchell, Mary; Schmidt, Marie. *Indian Reservations of Idaho, Oregon and Washington*. Portland Bureau of Indian Affairs, United States Department of the Interior, 1960.

MAGAZINES AND PERIODICALS

Arno, Stephen F. "The North Cascades," *National Parks Magazine*, June, 1967, pp. 2–9.

Brockman, C. Frank. "A Park for the North Cascades," *American Forests*, September, 1966, pp. 8–11, 50–52.

Brooks, Paul. "The Fight for America's Alps," *Atlantic*, February, 1967, pp. 87–99.

Brown, Gilbert. "The Romance of City Light," special supplement to *Seattle Star* Sunday Magazine, January 27, 1937.

Cleveland, Carl M. "Former Sheriff Bernard McCaulay was Tireless Foe of Bootleggers," *Okanogan Independent*, October 25, 1973.

Connelly, Dolly. "Mighty Joe Morovits, Real Life Bunyan," *Sports Illustrated*, January 7, 1963, pp. 52–57.

Connelly, Dolly. "Indians, Miners, Stockmen Blazed the Way," *Seattle Times*, July 10, 1960.

Cooper, Carl L. "The Skagit Story," special supplement to *Seattle Post-Intelligencer*, March 5, 1951.

Davis, Don. "How Skagit Valley Towns Came About," *Everett Herald* Magazine, October 16, 1971.

"Lumberjack's Sky Ride," *Popular Mechanics*, August, 1945, p. 71.

"Methods Used on Ross Dam by General-Shea-Morrison," *Pacific Builder and Engineer*, April, 1946.

Mitchell, Bruce. "By River, Trail and Rail," special supplement to *Wenatchee World* by Chelan County Industrial Development Council, September, 1968.

Murphy, Edward C. "Highway to Valhalla," *Washington Highways*, July, 1969, pp. 9–12.

Murray, Keith A. "Building a Wagon Road Through the Northern Cascade Mountains," *Pacific Northwest Quarterly*, April, 1965.

North Cascades Special Edition on North Cascades Highway, *Pacific Builder and Engineer*, September 1, 1972.

North Cascades Special Edition on North Cascades Highway, *Washington Highways*, September, 1972.

North Cascades Study Report, United States Government Printing Office.

Park, Edwards. "Washington Wilderness, the North Cascades," *National Geographic Magazine*, March, 1961, pp. 334–67.

Peck, William K. "Mountain Outfitter," *Tacoma News-Tribune and Sunday Ledger*, December 10, 1972.

Warner, Lowell. "Thunder Mountain Mines," *Sunday Olympian*, November 3, 1968.

Widrig, Charlotte. "Homesteading on the Upper Skagit Was a Rough but Interesting Life," *Seattle Times*, December 24, 1961.

Widrig, Charlotte. "Backwoods Groceryman Was Kept Busy," *Seattle Times*, December 31, 1961.

MANUSCRIPTS AND TYPESCRIPTS

Bellingham. Eldridge Carr personal papers and letters, at his residence.

Bellingham. Sig Hjaltalin scrapbook of North Cascades Highway Association activities, JoAnn Roe offices.

Bellingham. Bert Huntoon diary kept during North Cascades explorations, JoAnn Roe offices.

Bellingham. Keith Murray, "Historical Background of the North Cross-State Highway," paper given before the Hobby Club, Bellingham, 1961, JoAnn Roe offices.

Bellingham. John Pierce private papers, letters, and memoirs approximately 1950–72, at home of Martha Knowles, daughter.

Okanogan. Editions of Okanogan County Heritage, publications of Okanogan County Historical Society.

Olympia. State of Washington Public Documents, Committee of Public Lands Report, 1907–08.

Pateros. Private papers of Art Nordang at his residence.

Seattle. Archives of Mount Baker National Forest, Burton Babcock file.

Seattle. Archives of Seattle City Light. "March of Time on the Upper Skagit," typed memoirs of Doc Barbeau.

Seattle. Archives of Mount Baker National Forest. "The Mount Baker Almanac," compiled by Field, Newton, for United States Forest Service, typed manuscript.

Seattle. Archives of Mount Baker National Forest. "Early Skagit Recollections," Otto Klement, typed memoirs.

Seattle. Archives of Mount Baker National Forest. Memoirs of C. C. McGuire, typed.

Seattle. Archives of Mount Baker National Forest. Report on Skagit Queen Mines, 1908, Charles E. Phoenix, typed.

Seattle. Seattle City Light. Seattle City Light News, privately published newspaper, selected editions.

Seattle. University of Washington, Suzzallo Library, Northwest Collection, "The History of Skagit County," Violet Burmaster, unpublished manuscript, 1931.

Seattle. University of Washington, Suzzallo Library, Northwest Collection, "Early Historical Incidents of Skagit County," Ethel Van Vleet Harris, unpublished manuscript, 1932.

Seattle. University of Washington, Suzzallo Library, Northwest Collection, "A History of the Upper Skagit Valley, 1880–1924," Paul Curtis Pitzer, unpublished master's thesis, 1966.

Seattle. University of Washington, Suzzallo Library, Northwest Collection, "J. D. Ross and Seattle City Light," William O. Sparks, unpublished master's thesis, 1964.

Sedro Woolley. The Skagit Corporation, Dubuar scrapbook.

Washington, D.C. North Cascades Study Report, U.S. Government Printing Office.

Washington, D.C. U.S. Government Printing Office, "Report of An Expedition from Fort Colville to Puget Sound, Washington Territory, by way of Lake Chelan and Skagit River . . . August and September, 1882." Henry H. Pierce, typescript, 1883.

Washington, D.C. Office of History and Historic Architecture, Eastern Service Center, U.S. Department of the Interior, National Park Service, U.S. Government, "North Cascades National Park, Ross Lake N.R.A., and Lake Chelan, N.R.A., History Basic Data," by Erwin N. Thompson, paperback typescript, bound, March, 1970.

NEWSPAPERS

Of particular value to the research for *The North Cascadians* were three weekly newspapers: the *Mount Vernon Argus, Concrete Herald* and *Methow Valley News*. All have been in publication since the turn of the century and provided the initial clues to important happenings on both sides of the mountains. From the data base provided, the author was able to pursue events more closely to obtain personal interviews and insights.

Selected editions of the following newspapers were used in general research.

Anacortes American
Bellingham Bay Mail
Bellingham Herald
Bellingham Reveille
Brewster Herald
Burlington Farm Journal
Chelan Leader
Concrete Herald, 1901–72
Everett Herald

Methow Valley Journal
Methow Valley News
Mount Vernon Argus, 1891–1972
Northern Light
Okanogan Independent
Omak Chronicle
Puget Sounder, 1935–39 in the Northwest Collection, University of
    Washington, Seattle
Seattle Star, 1918–24
Skagit Valley Herald
Spokane Spokesman-Review
Wenatchee World, chiefly features by Hu Blonk, historical writer
    and former editor

PERSONAL INTERVIEWS

Jack Abrams	Richard Grantham	John Pierce
H. K. Anderson	Sig Hjaltalin	Bessie Pressentin
Emmett Aston	C. M. Hoidal	Mabel Pressentin
Bruno Benedetti	Lester Holloway	David Rahm
Sig Berglund	Victor Jacobsen	Francis Scarvie
Galen Biery	Ernest Johnson	Jessie Schmidt
Tom Black	Ed Kikendall	Jack Sherin
Hu Blonk	Ken King	Archie Shiels
Harold Bowers	Francis Lufkin	Dewey Smith
Thomas Bucknell	Fred Martin	Harriet Staack
Eldridge Carr	Catherine McClintock	Grace Clark Stafford
Harold Chriswell	Gordon McGovern	Ray Steiger
Glee Davis	David McIntyre, Jr.	Percy Stendal
Molly Dowdle	George Miller	Irwin Stokes
Edward Drobnack	Ivan Munson	Leonard Therriault
Cal Dunnell	Keith Murray	Wade Troutman
Clyde Ewell	John Nelson	Kathryn Wagner
Charlie Flagg	Mrs. K. M. Nelson	Elizabeth Widel
Robert French	Mrs. Ben Nickell	Hubert Wilson
Gerald Gannon	Art Nordang	Jack Wilson
Keith Gaston	Rod O'Connor	Bruce Zahn
Paul Gay	Dan Peterson	

Index

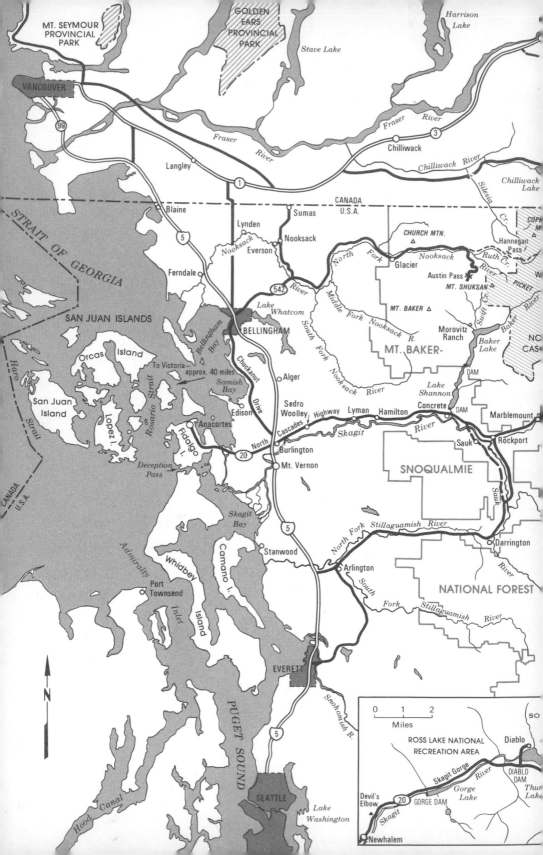